YOU ALL
LOOK ALIKE

YOU ALL
LOOK ALIKE
A Family Memoir

KRISTIN ELLIOTT

TABLE OF CONTENTS

PREFACE

ONE EVENING in my early twenties, I attended a lawn party in the Hamptons. Inexplicably, while chatting with total strangers, I was able to guess the number of siblings each person had in their family and even where each ranked in the order from oldest to youngest. I could guess who was an only child. Needless to say, I was the hit of the party. Despite whispers and jokes about witchcraft, that night I tapped into the potent way our families shape us. Without being aware of it, each of us sends out signals that reveal our identity. Were we the favorite? Or the black sheep? Did we have sisters and brothers? If the listener is tuned in . . . Bingo!

These eleven essays, which I also consider stories, reflect who I am today, an independent woman with a successful corporate career in the rearview mirror, pursuing writing in my retirement. While writing represents a path to self-knowledge, it also connects me to peers who have progressed along similar stepping stones to adulthood.

Did you ever wonder if your childhood was a predictor of who you'd become as an adult?

Often, I did. About two years ago, I considered writing down the stories of my formative years. I thought, maybe, in the telling, they'd build upon each other, giving me insights into later chapters of my life.

You All Look Alike is the result, a memoir of my childhood and adolescence in the late 1940s, 1950s, and early 1960s, growing up in Beverly, Massachusetts on the North Shore of Boston. This collection recounts family events that shaped me from the age of four to seventeen. Who of us hasn't struggled to differentiate ourselves, whether from a sister, a brother, or our friends? Adolescent rites of passage reflect a need for validation and love.

If my memories are flawed, I can count on my older sisters and brother to set me straight. Nevertheless, we each recall events differently because of when they happened and at what impressionable age we were when they occurred. Perspective also varies depending on sibling placement. What impacts one may leave little impression on another.

For me, being the youngest child may be the reason that I assumed the role of family storyteller. I worried about being left behind. Perhaps watching and listening to my brother and sisters, as well as to my parents, in order to keep up the pace, made me a keen observer and an attentive listener, traits that go hand-in-hand with the writing process.

I scurried to keep up, last among four closely spaced siblings—Susan, "Bud" (his nickname, but whose name is Charles Francis Elliott, Jr.), and Joan (spelled the Scottish way and pronounced Jo-Ann). Never, ever, was I a typical baby, indulged and pampered. Mine was a "don't let the canoes leave without me" mindset.

These stories represent a coming of age in America immediately after World War II and the decades beyond, a few months following the Cuban Missile Crisis. They acknowledge milestones in teenaged years that coincide with historic events, such as the presidential election of 1960 and the Massachusetts U.S. Senate race in 1962. They also hark back to a time when there was a strong sense of neighborhood, where children of all ages played Run, Sheep, Run and Kick the Can in streets empty at night after dinner. In the early 1950s, a bunch of teenagers within a six-block radius, along with children as young as first graders, mounted a talent show to raise monies for the local chapter of the Red Cross. Our many offerings included a ballet dance by my sister Susan; a high wire act on our tall swing set by my brother Bud; and harmonizing to the lyrics of "You're not sick, you're just in love," belted out by Joan and me. The event merited our photograph and a brief write-up in the *Beverly Evening Times*.

This memoir is also a salute to my hometown, Beverly, to this day battling the claim as the "Birthplace of the American Navy," with its archrival, the prestigious sailing capitol of the Northeast: Marblehead.

Equally, it's an homage to my parents, who made admirable decisions throughout their adult lives, whose choices empowered me to make a few of my own. And, lastly, it's an embrace of Susan, Bud, and Joan, without whom I'd be bereft.

Cherished family memories are what we pass on to future generations. *You All Look Alike* preserves a piece of our Elliott family narrative.

And guess what? We pretty much all still look alike.

9

A REMARKABLE MOTHER

IN THE MID-1930S, it must have been highly unusual for a single woman of barely twenty to get behind the wheel of a car to peddle farm products amid open fields, rolling hills, and acres of pastures. Yet this petite, perky woman had been given a wide geographical territory that covered Massachusetts and New Hampshire. I liked imagining my pretty mother, her fetching red lipstick calling attention to her dimples while she unpacked pots and pans from the trunk of her Ford car. My hunch? The Eastern States Farmers' Exchange (ESFE) had bet correctly that a diminutive home economist would generate sales of their utilitarian goods despite the hardships of the Depression.

"Wasn't I the lucky one during those hardscrabble times?" she told me.

My four-year-old imagination pictured her in the black two-door sedan she'd described, chugging up and down hilly roads in the White Mountains, or tooting past asparagus fields in western Massachusetts. While setting up her cooking demonstration in the exhibition tent, my mother would attract the attention of farmers. How could they resist pausing to get a whiff of her warm applesauce sprinkled with cinnamon? No doubt, she'd flash her radiant smile, reeling the men in. Then, she'd flirt a little with her sparkly blue eyes. She'd hold her breath, watching as a tight-fisted shopper dug his calloused fingers deep into his overall pockets to retrieve a worn greenback. The sale? A clunky metal apple corer that required attachment to a kitchen table. This gift would be quite the surprise for the wife greeting him after his excursion from home.

From the time I was perched in a highchair to the years I moved to the grown-up seat at the kitchen table, I'd been an eyewitness to Mom greeting the milkman and the fishmonger who came regularly to our kitchen back door. She clearly liked the men, addressing them by name, inquiring about their families. She'd listen intently, hands on hips, nodding, while they pattered about their children's progress in school. Often, they'd linger, as if reluctant to leave the warmth of a Betsy Worden Elliott kitchen. And the warmth of her bright smile.

Mom often recalled her happy memories to me. One afternoon, she noted with pride that she'd paid her college tuition working as a cook with little prior experience. "I worked my way through tiny Massachusetts State College," (unrecognizable today as the huge University of Massachusetts) "cooking for my sorority," Mom said. "Good thing I was a quick learner. Breakfast was a cinch, pulling down cereal boxes and grabbing milk bottles out of the fridge for sorority sisters. Dinner? More challenging. Your grandmother Worden had given me the

Fanny Farmer Cookbook. As you know, my dear, I am still a fan of this kitchen bible. Guess what? Every sorority sister ate heartily. No one complained," she said, glancing down to catch my eye as she brushed an errant curl from her flushed face.

Watching her finger go down the ingredients checklist on the dog-eared pot roast recipe page, I relished the storytelling that animated her face. What an amazing way to tap her sorority cooking expertise! She continued by stating that it wasn't such a big leap to go from cooking for sorority sisters to demonstrating practical products to hard-working farmers. She never confessed to being lost or afraid while driving about uncharted territory, that I recall. And no matter that I'd heard this story often, I never tired of it. What a marvel, my mother, the older sibling in her family, galivanting all over New England to help pay her brother's tuition at Tufts Dental School. "During the Depression, that's what family did," Mom said.

I was amazed to learn how Mom had worked four years after college to support her family, particularly her brother John. And subsequently, how she and my father agreed to postpone their marriage. Those years in the 1930s, called the Great Depression, had imprinted forever in my parents' memories. My parents explained how starving families had stood in long bread lines; hoboes had lived in tented camps; and unemployed men had jumped aboard trains for unknown cities in search of work. Thankfully, the Depression was over long before I was born.

Inhaling the rich aroma of Mom's simmering onions for a beef stew, I was glad not to have an ache in my stomach while awaiting a meager bowl of soup and a slice of bread. At the same time, I was sure that my oldest sister, Susan, was not going to be paying my way through college. The nightmare of the Depression had lifted after World War II and the economic boom of the 1950s. By then, the average family owned a car, and single-family homes were being constructed on empty lots and former farmland.

Hanging around Mom as she organized dinner for our family of six was one of my favorite rituals, what with my three older siblings ensconced in Hardie School up the street. Our yellow and white kitchen gleamed from Mom's vigilant sponge. The yellow and black speckled linoleum floor complemented the yellow Formica and stainless-steel kitchen table with its six matching chairs. Smooth white steel cabinets opened up to stacks of aluminum pots and pans as well as many Eastern States Farmers' Exchange utensils. Mom's meatloaf, pot roast, roast beef, or ham might be transformed the following day into hash or patties, thanks to the ESFE meat grinder. Cleaning as she went about her business, Mom would let me step up on a stool to rinse a bowl or a measuring cup. That task gave me a moment to sneak a lick of the brownie batter with a practiced index finger.

When I think about Mom, it's most often when I'm in my kitchen. Much of what I learned about cooking came from shadowing her, watching her move efficiently from the electric Mixmaster to the generous refrigerator, to the oven, stopping to wash dishes in the white sink. She'd glide between General Electric appliances in her starched apron, humming an Ella Fitzgerald song, while orchestrating dinner. Like her, my *Fanny Farmer* has been my "go to" cookbook.

In childhood, I'd pull out the family photo album to stare at the black and white Kodak picture of Mom and Dad immediately after a snowstorm. Mom's brunette hair was falling softly to her shoulders, almost reaching her beaver coat, a hand-me-down fur from her beloved Aunt Ruth. What really stood out was Dad's long arm around her shoulder, drawing her close. His lanky, athletic body towered over her diminutive five foot two inches. A thick lock of his curly black hair gave him a dashing air. I'd seen them look at each other like this. Was Dad telling her that he felt like he'd won the trifecta at the horse races when he met her on a blind date in college? Was she delighting him by claiming he was the best-looking man she'd ever met? I would run my small index finger over the shiny image, staring, willing them to speak. Why were they gazing so deeply into each other's eyes? Even at age four, I could feel the electricity between them.

Dad had graduated two years ahead of Mom and enrolled in Harvard Medical School. Despite their devotion to each other, getting married was out of the question. Mom reminded all four of us kids, "Dad was in medical school, as was Uncle John. That meant I needed a reliable job with a steady income." She smiled, probably remembering the many sales she'd rung up while being a New England sales rep for ESFE.

When Dad was in Cambridge at medical school, he taught her to drive, a prerequisite for her unusual job opportunity. This amused all four of us Elliott kids growing up. Often, we teased Mom about her sense of direction, or the lack of it. We observed how Dad automatically got behind the wheel when they drove together or with all of us as a family. How had she managed to find her way from town to village on poorly marked New England backroads? I was even more puzzled when designated the family navigator because of my excellent long-range vision and map-reading skills. Was it her smile and grit that got her from A to Z? Like the proverbial postman who wasn't deterred by rain, snow, or sleet, Mom made it to her exhibitions no matter how unfamiliar the location. I pictured her grabbing a freshly ironed apron to tie a perky bow behind her slim waist. Of course, she'd run a brush through her wavy hair. And, with a last flourish, with no need for a mirror, she'd apply the dash of her Revlon Fire and Ice red lipstick.

"A woman never ventures out without a fresh application," she noted. "You don't know who you'll bump into. Best to look your best." To this day, I heed her advice, taking the extra seconds to swipe my lips before greeting my public.

Once, while fingering the starched bow of her apron, I wondered out loud if Mom and Dad were sad that they had to wait four years before marrying. Mom explained, "Everyone made personal sacrifices during the Depression. Dad and I saw each other most weekends, of course. He was in Boston while I was in West Springfield, only three hours away. When we did marry, we were ready to start our family. Susan came right away, followed by Bud. Then a slight pause before Joan." She laughed. "You, my dear," tapping me lightly on the nose, "were the surprise. From top to bottom, four babies within four and a half years. Lots of diapers. We decided four was enough."

I sighed with relief. What if they had stopped at three with my sister, Joan, not quite a full year older than me? My imagination was vivid yet could not grapple with the concept that I wouldn't be here now, next to Mom, breathing in her favorite cologne, Chanel No. 5, if they had somehow stopped at three. I wouldn't be part of our family. I wouldn't be throwing balls to Brandy, our frisky wire-haired Fox Terrier. I wouldn't be chasing after Susan, Bud, and Joan, yelling at them to slow down. I wouldn't be laughing over the dinner chatter. I wouldn't be . . . well, that was the point. It was unfathomable. I only knew how much fun it was to have three older siblings to look up to, to keep up to. Playing catch up, not being left behind. I admired all of them and never wanted them to dismiss me as the baby in the family. Not a baby, never was, never will be, I pledged silently. I was part of this family. There was no way I could not be me. Or not be. No way.

To us sisters, Mom passed on a homily or two, in addition to the lipstick admonition. Susan, my oldest sister, was smart enough to skip a grade, despite being small for her age. When she stood at the blackboard making a presentation in the fourth grade for parent's day, my mother proclaimed that she was "grown up, almost an adult." I am confident that Mom said nothing like that about me when I reached that nine-year-old milestone. Mom admired brains and poise, both of which Susan possessed in amplitude. Mom also was social, chatting easily with both men and women. Like her, Joan had a ready smile and laugh.

"Watch how easily Joan mingles with others," Mom would whisper in my ear. In a ten-minute line of strangers, Joan would have a new best friend in five minutes. "Why not mimic her?" Clearly, Joan had learned to imitate Mom, taking mental notes as Mom chit-chatted with the fishmonger and the Hood's milkman.

As outgoing as Joan was, I was introverted. Painfully shy. My quiet father would listen as Mom replayed a chance meeting at Givonni's grocery store with the owner of our local funeral home, Lee & Moody. "When Bill Moody tells me I've never looked better, I do not take it as a compliment," she joked. My father chuckled. "Rather," she continued, with an appreciative nod toward Dad, "I worry that mortician is prospecting for his next customer." Dad stood tall, arms crossed, never interrupting. To console myself, I decided I was more akin to my stoic father. I'll be like him, I told myself. Joan could be like Mom.

Shortly before my parents married, Dad had to pull out of medical school. He had struggled with a debilitating case of trichinosis, thanks to a landlady who had not cooked a pork roast fully. (And he was never much a fan of pork afterwards.) He'd been so ill that he flunked organic chemistry. Afterward, he'd fared poorly in a summer make-up course at Boston University. It was the end of a dream. I always wondered how much this failure impacted him. With his sensitivity and compassion, he'd have been a wonderful physician. What I did know was that, despite his deep disappointment, he recognized he had to earn a living. As he often said, he had to "get the show on the road."

Getting full-time work in the 1930s was challenging. Dad accepted part-time positions, one as a Fuller Brush salesman. This job was not a good match for my introverted father, even though I was fairly sure that my outgoing mother could have sold brushes to bald men. Eventually, he landed a plum engineering position in radio tubes with Sylvania Electric in Lynn, a city a few miles north of Boston. Apparently, the abstract thinking involved in engineering is similar to what's required for doctors. His "critical skills" designation at Sylvania meant he would not be enlisted in World War II.

Here is their history as I remember the retelling. Well before my dad had the Sylvania job, he and Mom had married, in both a civil ceremony and in the Catholic Church, to appease his religious mother. Then, they began having babies, quickly and easily. Meanwhile, Mom was working part-time in a Lynn gift shop. As the war was winding down, Sylvania asked Dad to relocate to Scranton, Pennsylvania. Ever the dyed-in-the-wool New Englander, Dad balked. At home, he muttered that Scranton was in the middle of a cultural desert and only known for coal mines. I'd heard him quote former Supreme Court Justice Oliver Wendell Holmes who called Boston "the Hub of the Universe." Undoubtedly, Dad did not mention this reference when he formally turned down the relocation offer. Luckily, his supervisor liked him. He would not be penalized for refusing to relocate. Then again, I wondered, who didn't like my soft-spoken father?

Both Mom and Dad shared a strong streak of independence. Neither wanted to work a lifetime for a company or for a government agency. They wanted to be the decision-makers, unlike their fathers. Grandpa Elliott had been a city policeman living in the Boston suburb of Waltham. Grandpa Worden had held a variety of jobs in western Massachusetts: in a paper mill, in an ice factory, and as a machinist motorman. While all these blue-collar jobs provided some measure of security or pensions, they did not require great intellect or leadership skills from men who possessed them. My guess? My parents opted not to go the conventional route. Rather, they pursued a mutual venture that would introduce them to unknown opportunities.

Together, Mom and Dad concocted a scheme for the enterprise they'd build together. Her experience in the Lynn retail shop led them to calculate how greeting cards sold briskly per square foot while not requiring much floor space. My mother was intrigued that holiday cards sold quickly as well. She liked a small New England line of cards called Red Farm Studios. Neither of them cared for the flowery rhymes and poems inside the cards of the industry giants, American Greetings and Hallmark. My parents believed there might be room for a card line with a keen eye for realistic artwork without cringeworthy sentimentality. With few savings, four infants, and plenty of gumption, they founded a greeting card company as equal business partners. Rather than compete with the bigger names in the card industry, they carved out a specialty niche: Christmas cards. The timing was shortly after my birth. Thinking that Kristin and Christmas sounded alliterative— indeed, memorable—they named the company Kristin Elliott Christmas Cards.

Soon, the basement of our three-bedroom white clapboard Garrison home was crammed floor to ceiling with cartons of holiday cards and crisp, white envelopes and red boxes, sitting above the cement floor on wooden slats to stay dry. Every possible theme was represented: New England snow-covered bridges, green wreaths, Santa Claus with his sleigh, angels and crèches, and iconic Christmas trees surrounded by bountiful gifts.

The artists who designed the cards were from the greater Boston area initially, as the company established itself. In the early days of getting up and running, word-of-mouth was like networking today. One artist would tell another that a new card company needed to buy original designs for $35 each. Coming home from school from the first to the twelfth grades, I'd arrive to find an artist on the sofa with designs spread out over our two big, hooked rugs. "What do you think of this crèche scene?" Hattie Wentworth of Rockport would ask. I'd guffaw as she pointed out a small pig near the baby Jesus, knowing she'd had a pet pig when she was a little girl. "I always sneak a piglet in," she'd confess. "No one seems to mind." How thrilling for me, being in-the-know.

Another time, I'd returned from Beverly High School to see Mom huddled on the sofa next to Beatrice Stone, who lived in the Cove section of Beverly. Mom would save clippings from magazines like *The New Yorker* or *The Saturday Evening Post.* When Beatrice said, "I'm not sure what you mean by inserting a Christmas tree behind the angel, Betsy," Mom located the right scrap of paper to illustrate her point. Voilà! A light bulb went off. This happened often. The finished art would capture what my mother was looking for and become a potential bestseller.

That was upstairs business, usually including a hearty home-made dinner with the entire family. Downstairs, in the alcove by the bottom of the cellar steps, stood an imposing metal linotype printing press. It was huge, with long black arms and legs that resembled an elephant. It seemed to reach from floor to ceiling of the basement, towering over every carton, box, and shelf. How I loved the smell of the greasy ink and the *thwap, thwap* of the shiny wheel as Dad foot-peddled it. The glorious, red-inked letters, as if by magic, but really by my father's hand, imprinted a customer name inside each greeting card. This was the personalized part of the greeting card business, having one's name imprinted inside the card and under "Seasons Greetings" or "Merry Christmas and a Happy New Year." No saccharine poetry, no sickeningly sweet sentiment inside a Kristin Elliott Christmas Card.

I'd watch as Dad counted out loud: Five, ten, fifteen, twenty, twenty-five. If it was a decent order, the customer would order 200 cards separated into bright red boxes of twenty-five in each, with the white Kristin Elliott logo over it in my mother's handwriting. Oddly enough, years later, my handwriting was almost identical to hers.

Dad's personal imprinting of card orders seemed like a kind of holiday miracle to a child. I'd watch him move the letter type around, spelling the names out loud to proofread them against the buyers' orders before applying the water-based ink. Then, he'd press the peddle to start another personal order for another boutique gift shop. Unlike other fathers, Dad found time to pitch in and help Mom around the house with chores like vacuuming and the kitchen dishes. One year, my sister Susan told her fourth-grade teacher that her father did not go to work. No, she insisted, he grabbed a cup of coffee and disappeared down the cellar stairs every morning. On parent's night, her concerned teacher wished my father good luck finding a job.

Those early years in a start-up business required Dad to return for short stints at Sylvania, temporary work that his supervisor was kind enough to offer him to "get over a hump." No surprise, then, that Mom assumed an ongoing freelance assignment from her former employer, the Farmers' Exchange. But this assignment was different, not requiring time away from home and family, not selling pots and pans. Instead, monthly, she prepared an article for the members' magazine with accompanying photo spreads. Hours before the New Hampshire-based freelance photographer pulled into our Dane Street driveway, she'd review the checklist and assemble cookie sheets, spatulas, mixing bowls, and ingredients on countertops. The aroma of Parker House rolls fresh from a hot oven or custard-filled chocolate eclairs cooling by the open window let the photographer, Gordon Herndon, know he was expected. It didn't take long for the faces of neighborhood kids to peer through the screen window, noses poised like hunting dogs catching the scent. Betsy Elliott's cooking prowess was well established before I reached first grade.

Sometimes, if one of the handful of regional sales reps was unable to pay a call on a potential buyer, Mom would pitch in. The business was too small to pay the salary of a full-time salesperson. She and Dad would let the rep know that one of them would make the sales call and still give him his commission. When Susan, Bud, and Joan were in class at Hardie, she might suggest that the two of us go into Boston for a small adventure.

One morning, hand in hand, me in my sandals and sundress, her in high heels and shirtwaist dress, we boarded the Amtrak train for the thirty-five-minute ride to North Station to walk the short distance to the Women's Exchange gift shop on Boylston Street. There, she introduced herself to the head buyer and brought out her Kristin Elliott Christmas Cards portfolio. I stood by shyly, fidgeting with the ribbon on my pigtails.

"What is the name of your little carbon copy with the big blue eyes?" the buyer inquired. I blushed.

"This is the real Kristin Elliott, for whom Charlie and I named the business."

The buyer stared, charmed. She seemed as impressed as if making the acquaintance of Lady Hallmark of Hallmark cards (the biggest name in the card business even then). No surprise, by bringing in the Real McCoy, Mom had nailed down a bigger than anticipated order.

Over the years, I got a kick out of having the family business named for me. How special to meet a stranger in Chicago who thought my name sounded familiar, only to trace it to her being a card buyer in Montgomery Ward. Or, to chat with the owner of a bookstore who was a devotee of our specialty line. Or, to meet someone who repeated my name, saying it sounded musical, memorable. Then, suddenly, she'd connect the dots and reveal that she always sought out Kristin Elliott Christmas Cards over the holidays.

Susan, Joan, and I assisted my mother by doing the entries of orders in their business books as well as with the filing. We had first-hand familiarity with customers across the country, from bookshops to department stores, Christmas shops to high-end boutiques. When I was at Wellesley College, a dorm friend returned from the local Hathaway House Bookshop with a red box of cards. She tossed the box my way. "A gift for you! I had to buy them because your name is written all over the box!" Once, on a bareboat sailing charter in the Caribbean, a shipmate who ran a gift shop in Wisconsin said my name rang a bell. When I suggested the connection, she insisted her husband take a photo of us. "Wait 'til my co-workers see me with you. They'll be jealous and thrilled to learn that you were on the high seas with me."

The ubiquitous red boxes with my name in white script were always my secret source of pride as a child, adolescent, and adult. Did I ever ask my siblings if they were jealous? For some reason, no. Did Susan, Bud, or Joan express resentment? Not that I remember. Eventually, it would be Bud who took over the family business when my parents talked about succession and retirement.

Sibling rivalry about the business never came into play. Susan had a strong identity as Number One in our lineup. Bud had inherited Dad's athleticism. And, despite the fact my family treated boys and girls as equals, he was the only boy. Joan? She was the lovable softie. Like Susan and Bud, I never heard her complain about not being endowed with the business' name. My parents' rationale for how they'd decided upon it seemed to suffice.

Of course, I'd done nothing to deserve the designation. Still, it was a point of separation from my siblings. Decades later, when my brother Bud was buying the business, he considered changing the name to Charles Elliott, Inc. However, market research advised against switching from an existing, well-established brand name. I breathed a big sigh of relief.

Despite being shy, I secretly cherished my name and having a business named with it. It took until my early years in the corporate world to mingle easily in mixed company. My professional career in advertising, public relations, and marketing depended on working a room to succeed. Nothing like learning on the job.

Deep inside, the magic of being Kristin Elliott of Kristin Elliott Christmas Cards always made me feel extra special.

BUTTERSCOTCH OR CHOCOLATE

IN MY BEVERLY HIGH SCHOOL eleventh-grade English class, Helena Corbett waggled her arthritic finger in my direction. "Charlie!"

I groaned inwardly. That was my brother Bud's given name. And there was no student in the classroom with the name Charles. I was the last of us Elliotts to sit in her class, reading Robert Frost poems and learning ten new "Word Wealth" vocabulary words a week. It occurred to me that this woman's eyesight or brains might be failing. Maybe both. Clearly, she was not mistaking me for either of my two older sisters. Making matters worse, to my teenaged embarrassment, she barked out "Charlie" again, still staring at me. My cheeks got hot as I sank lower into my unforgiving wooden chair.

I piped up, slowly, unwillingly, "Mrs. Corbett, by any chance do you mean me? Kristin?"

She harrumphed. "Well, no wonder I got confused. Anyone can see that all you Elliotts look exactly alike."

Of course, we did resemble each other. But what sixteen-year-old girl wants to be told that she looks exactly like her brother? We all inherited a mixture of Scottish, Irish, and English genes. We had fair Celtic skin that, if we were lucky, freckled in the sun. Growing up when Johnson's Baby Oil took preference over suntan lotion, we often got sunburns. Bud's exposed nose peeled many times over the summer, enough that we teased him for having a natural red beacon. Thanks to Norah Hurley (Dad's mother) and her County Roscommon heritage, combined with the Cattanaugh genealogy (Mom's mother) from Scotland, our hair color varied little, from almost black to brunette. Of course, for all of us kids to possess the recessive genes for blue eyes, both parents also had to have blue eyes. When people remarked on how similar we all looked, they often singled me out for having the most piercing blue eyes, the color of aquamarine.

In a 1951 photograph, with the four of us lining up on the brick front stoop at 57 Dane Street, we resembled stepping stones, top to bottom: Susan, eleven; Bud, nine; Joan, seven; and me, six. Susan's generous smile shows off even teeth (a nod to braces) and compliments her wavy brown hair. Bud, shorter, but not for much longer, has an impish grin, in sync with his straight brown whiffle cut. Lots of freckles. He got the nickname "Bud" from Mom and Dad because he was a junior, Charles Francis Elliott, Jr. Neither parent wanted him to be called Junior, and my father was called Charlie. Thus, they picked the nickname Bud for him. As for Joan, she boasted soft brown curls that highlighted her winsome smile. Her first name was in honor of my mother's Scottish grandmother, a strong, independent woman who pronounced this spelling as "Jo-Ann." For most of her life, Joan has needed to set the record straight on the proper pronunciation of her name. In the seventh grade, she attempted to change it by writing it phonetically on her paperwork, but her teacher did not approve. Me? I was Joan's height, only shooting an inch higher in my teens. My name was often mispronounced as well, as if I were the Danish author Hans Christian Andersen. Today, Kristin is a well-established name. Not so in the early 1950s. Sometimes I was assigned to boys gym class. As for my hair color, my straight dark bangs, often disciplined by a demanding barrette, resembled my dad's black hair.

The English class episode was unusual. I was more accustomed to being confused with and compared to my sister, Joan. Before grade school, we were inseparable. I was one week shy of being born exactly on the same day as she was: My birthday is October third, while Joan's is October tenth. Did my parents decide we might as well be twins? Otherwise, why dress us for our first seven years as if we were? When Mom's fingers were not flying over the Underwood manual typewriter keyboard creating Kristin Elliott Christmas Card invoices, they were edging cotton McCall's patterns under the needle of the Singer treadle sewing machine. The *drada-drad-drat* of the machine could quickly stitch two green-and-red plaid skirts with wide straps, one for Joan, and one for me. At night, Mom might relax by pulling out her steel knitting needles and skeins of bright yarn. She could create the back of a red cable cardigan sweater while watching the Ed Sullivan and Jimmy Durante television shows on a Sunday night. Of course, the same red woolen cardigan with its pretty cable pattern would soon have a duplicate. Our white shirts with matching Peter Pan colors completed our identical outfits, even down to our brown tie-up shoes from Alcon's Shoe Store in downtown Beverly.

Happily, we both wore out our identical skirts, blouses, smocked dresses, and quilted jumpers at the same time. No hand-me-downs for me!

Even if others could not, as a child, I could see obvious differences between Joan and me. Her wispy curls and sweet smile captivated strangers. "What an easy-going little girl!" they might gush. With me, it was my piercing eyes. "Oh, my, those eyes don't miss a trick," they might observe. However, by dressing us identically, Mom blurred the lines between our differences. People who glanced at us saw only our similarities. We liked to play it up for the seven days in October when we were actually the same chronological age. "Guess how old she is? How old I am?" And the kicker of course was, "Do you think we are twins?"

No wonder acquaintances and neighbors would shake their heads, peer down, and pause before answering our mischievous query. "You must be. You dress and look the same. You say you are the same age. Well, then, of course!"

We'd poke each other in the ribs, chortling. "We're not! We are Irish twins!" We'd hasten to add that was the magical week in October when we were the same age, so we could claim twinship for seven days.

How delighted we were to dupe people for that one week of the year before we set the record straight. We didn't know that the term "Irish twin" was—and still is—derogatory, implying that Irish bumpkins wasted no time having sex immediately after the breast-feeding mother came home with her newborn. My father vividly recalled a time in the 1930s when all Help Wanted ads said, "Irish need not apply." This put-down of

Irish over-sized families came from that same anti-Irish immigrant sentiment. My parents never discussed this term with us; to this day, I'm unsure whether they knew about our "Irish twin" shenanigans during the first week of October. Back then, Joan and I were innocents. Little did we know that the joke was on us.

Over the years, Joan fell into playing the role of surrogate mother to me. She was the Mother Hen, tut-tutting while shielding me under her protective wing. One day, my first-grade teacher, Miss Hollingshead, asked me to remain behind the class for a minute to have a private chat. I waited until the room was empty before stepping up slowly to her large wooden desk. She leaned down from her swivel desk chair and whispered, "You know what I'd like for Christmas, Kristin?"

I was horrified, wondering if our family could afford whatever item she was about to request. I was pretty sure she was not going to say, "a tin of your mother's fabulous moist brownies," or "those homemade chocolate chip cookies she made for Miss. Cluff when Joan had her last year." No, this sounded ominous, like maybe she'd want a pin from Desjardin's, or a dress from Webber's Department Store.

My throat was dry as I continued to stare at her. She continued, "I want you to find your voice. To speak up. You are a quiet little mouse."

I ran from the room all the way home, across the dusty path that cut through the lawn of the Beverly Commons, past the Hale Street stop sign and down to Dane Street, panting. As I slammed the front door shut behind me, Joan looked up from reading *Cherry Ames, Student Nurse*. She immediately placed it on the floor. Hugging me close to her body, she said, "What's wrong? Why are you out of breath?"

29

When I described what had happened, Joan stomped her foot. She pumped her arms up and down. Her face got beet red. "How dare she! That's not nice. What she said. Or, what she asked."

I wiped my eyes, nodding my head. Grateful she understood.

"Look, I've got a surefire way to make yourself feel better. It's my secret, but I'm willing to share." She pointed to the inside of her elbow, the patch of skin there. "Give it a whiff. It always smells good, like a baby's head. Afterwards, switch to the top of your arm. Rub your nose over it. I call it fuzzing my arm. The soft hair on your arm tickles your nose. And smells wonderful. In a few seconds, you've given yourself a hug."

I did as instructed. She was right! I felt better. She winked before embracing me. For many years, fuzzing my arm had a consistent, soothing effect, good advice from Joan, who knew the surprising comfort of the hair on top of her arm and the sweet essence inside the crook of her elbow. My Mother Hen had literally taken me under her wing. However, her caring advice did not cure my youthful reticence. Miss Hollingshead did not get her wished-for gift that Christmas.

Snapshots from adolescence reveal me, the admiring onlooker, gazing at Joan. In one, she is buttoning up my cardigan. My tiny fist is clenched. Why? In another, my best friend Huntly sits on the grass, trousered legs splayed toward the camera. Joan and I bookend her. I'm serious, unsmiling, clutching a bunch of fresh flowers from my mother's garden. Joan is beaming. A third Brownie photo records Joan, pouring water from a pitcher into the concrete birdbath in our backyard. I regard her as if she's St. Francis, dispersing blessings to our feathered friends. Everything my sister did seemed easy, spontaneous. I was more timid.

No matter what age we were turning, Mom made sure that all of us kids' birthdays were extra special. We did not have a lot of money to go out to restaurants. Dad pointed out that six was a big multiple. "It adds up quickly at dinner," he'd say. And we knew that Mom's cooking was as good, if not better, than any food at a restaurant.

In the 1950s, there were not that many restaurants to pick from. In fact, families rarely went out to eat mid-week. On a weekend, occasionally, grown-ups might splurge and go to dinner before playing bridge with friends. But it was not the norm.

During my childhood, Beverly had a McDonald's, one of the first in the country, down by Beverly Harbor. It was strictly fast food. We also had a Chinese restaurant that my father disliked immensely. "That's not food," he'd say. Dunkin' Donuts was a small coffee and donut chain, based solely in the Boston area. North Beverly boasted another family chain, too, which was based in Quincy, Massachusetts, Howard Johnson's. It was a rare treat when we filed in to order the fried food that we loved, even my father, who'd learned to hate fish after years of Catholic Friday night dinners featuring the odd parts of grotesque fish. At Howard Johnson's, we'd salivate, pointing to the pictures on the plastic menus of fried clams and French fries. We'd smack our lips as we pondered which flavor of ice cream from the twenty-eight choices to devour for dessert afterwards. For Dad, it was always chocolate. I never recall him picking another flavor. He was the same way with Mom, his one and only. As we closed the door behind HoJo's, we knew that we wouldn't return for several months.

Although going out for a birthday dinner was not a family tradition and there were few tempting places worth consideration, my parents made sure that ticking off another birthday would be memorable. Importantly, Mom would set the dining room table with her finest china. It was Spode, with a pretty pink and blue floral design. Out would come the blue linen tablecloth with matching napkins that she'd stitched up on her sewing machine. And her sterling silver, one of her wedding gifts. As a birthday girl, I did not have to set the table. Naturally, Mom would cook a delicious roast dinner. Each year, I was allowed to invite a close friend.

We'd even mark the occasion, much like Thanksgiving or Christmas, by placing an arrangement of green olives stuffed with pimentos into a porcelain plate that Aunt Ruth had given my mother. Everyone in my family had a huge appetite for olives, to the point that we counted—and remembered—how many each of us had consumed the last time we'd served them. If anyone had been shy by one, we'd compensate for it at the next special gathering. We inherited a good memory from our father.

The conclusion of the dinner? The birthday designate got to choose his or her flavor of sauce for the ice cream and cake finale. In late September, Mom would ask me for my preferred ice cream topping: butterscotch or chocolate.

"Chocolate," I'd shout, clapping my hands. Chocolate sauce, created and warmed on the stove, full of chocolate squares, butter, milk, vanilla extract, and sugar was my number one favorite. Butterscotch, full of butter, milk, and brown sugar, was a close second. Seven days later, Mom would turn to Joan and ask her the same question. Joan always said, "Butterscotch!" I liked that I got to choose before my older sister, since the birthday calendar tapped me before her. Of course, it was a moot point. Both of us knew we could count on the other to get our second favorite topping within the week. We were in it together.

My mouth watered as the warm sauce slithered over the cold mountain of vanilla ice cream scoops. Large pools of rich chocolate or sweet butterscotch melted the ice cream as it cascaded down in a rush to the bottom of the bowl. Suddenly, as the sauce cooled, it hardened and crackled. Just how I liked it. My tongue, my teeth, and my stomach ached with anticipation.

This birthday ritual continued until Joan left for college in the fall of 1962. Irish twins then . . . Irish twins forever.

MY ADOPTED FRIEND

ONE SPRING MORNING in 1950, the phone's sharp ring interrupted my playing with my paper dolls. Mom handed the black receiver to me. As we exchanged looks, I noted her ready smile and sparkling blue eyes. "Kristin, no surprise at all. It's Huntly, asking for you."

"I'll be right over," I promised my soul mate, my close neighbor only eight months younger than I was. Mom pointed at the woolen cardigan draped over a chair as I dashed out the back door. "Be home before dark," she called after my fleeing form. "It's your turn to set the table."

I was thrilled that Huntly had invited me over, as our house was quiet with my older sisters and brother up the street attending Hardie School. If I was jealous of their dinner chatter about teachers, classmates, and friends, I refused to admit it. My turn, next year, I comforted myself.

My Beverly, Massachusetts neighborhood encompassed six blocks sprawling out in three directions, a mixture of single-family homes, duplexes, and an occasional triple decker, twenty-two miles north of Boston. This collection of short side streets meandered slightly downhill to the town lawn that introduced a public beach and the Atlantic Ocean. On any given day, I could scrunch my sneakers into the rocky sand and throw my arms out against the salt air, breathing its briny scent deep into my lungs. There was always a tableau of water traffic, from sailboats to oil tankers minding the buoys as they navigated into the channel entrance between Beverly and Salem Harbors. Salty sailors had an expression: "red right returning." While standing on shore, it was fun to watch all the boats keep the bright red buoys to their starboard side when headed into harbor from open sea. I'd squint and try to conjure up the coast of England beyond the horizon. But try as I might, even my childhood imagination could not make out the famous White Cliffs of Dover.

Among our pre and postwar modest houses was one vacant lot filled with wild brush and weeds. Naturally, it was a magnet for Hide 'n Seek games. It was disappointing when a developer began pouring a concrete basement for a new home. Hale Street, the major thoroughfare a half-block up from our lower portion of Dane Street, merited a four-way stop for cars. Below that stop sign, kids of all ages could run free at night, once fathers pulled Ford station wagons and Dodge sedans into their garages, following the loud blast from the horn signaling the end of the workday at the local United Shoe Machinery Company. Summers, after supper, these streets provided the game board for Hopscotch; Run, Sheep, Run; and Kick the Can.

We created human shortcuts within this multi-street neighborhood. To get to Huntly's, I squeezed my small body between the privet hedge that marked the boundary between us and our back-door neighbors, a spinster (what single women were called then), and her mother who lived with a beloved cat, Sneakers. Sipping tea with Esther and Jane while petting Sneakers was a grown-up outing with Mom that I enjoyed. This morning, I hopped over their flagstone path to spill into Bancroft Circle, a U-shaped street with eight neat clapboard homes built before World War II. After a long stretch of wire fencing, Huntly's house loomed large. It fronted Hale Street at the far side of the circle, anchoring others with its sheer size and stature. The tall three-story colonial would have been notable in any town in Massachusetts or, for that matter, all New England. A Beverly Historic Society sign designated its heritage: Hale Farm, built in 1694. The sign is still there, marking the structure's remarkable preservation.

This sprawling mansion was (and still is) a living museum, boasting twelve-over-twelve windowpanes on the first and second stories, with small windows peeking from upstairs dormers. In addition to its many windows, other colonial symbols underlined its prosperous status: additions and ells; a hand-carved wooden pineapple over the front door; several brick chimneys. All architectural decorative elements signified that the original owner had been a man of means.

Fittingly, the first occupant was the highly regarded Reverend John Hale, a Puritan pastor. He became infamous, however, as prosecutor during the Salem witch trials in the last decade of the seventeenth century. During the hysteria, women and girls were accused, imprisoned, tried, and often burned at the stake for dealings with the Devil. The Reverend Hale's enthusiastic participation ended abruptly when his wife was accused of being a sorceress. Over several decades and centuries, as family fortunes waxed and waned, the Hale land holdings diminished. Fields that had flowed to the ocean eventually shrank to a single wooded acre. Even so, the mansion stood uncontested as the most significant structure in town.

Late in the 1800s, at least one Hale descendent was forced to convert a large ell that fronted on Hale Street into a carriage trade bookshop. The Hale House Bookshop sign served as an advertising billboard, catching the eye of the Boston Brahmins clip-clopping by to escape hot city temperatures for cooler breezes along the North Shore, headed for towns like Pride's Crossing, Manchester-by-the-Sea, and Magnolia. It was romantic to picture them perusing the plentiful stock of hardcover books. These classic reads would make wonderful companions with which to wile away the hours in rocking chairs on cottage porches with commanding views of the Atlantic.

Huntly and I enjoyed roaming Hale Farm's warren of rooms while speculating about its former inhabitants. Had they feared neighbors, worried they might turn on them, declaring them in cahoots with the Devil? Tiptoeing over worn, wooden floorboards, we heard the uneven 250-year-old planks groan underfoot. We'd shut a warped door only to jump at its squeaky protest. Was the house whispering about its past? I cocked an ear. Was it spooked because its early dwellers had been accused of sorcery? Was it warning us that history sometimes repeats itself? Had we listened better would we have heard? Or understood? We worried that we could have been burned at the stake for being miniature witches. We preferred pretending that we were princesses in search of Prince Charming, but we always came back to the horrors of witchcraft.

Huntly's mother had an arrangement with the Beverly Historic Society to open Hale Farm to the public on selective days in the summer in exchange for managing its bookshop. She could keep all the book sales revenue if she allowed the public a few days' access to this amazing historic building. Fortunately, the family's bedrooms were off limits. Huntly would hug her stuffed dog close, saying, "No one gets near Mr. Puggles. No one can touch him!"

We didn't mind the occasional rainy day because her cavernous home boasted nooks and crannies ideal for exploration. It was a treasure trove for two imaginative four-year-old girls.

"Lunch time," Huntly's mother, Martha, called up the back stairs. The sweet aroma of oatmeal raisin cookies wafted through the floorboards up into Huntly's bedroom. Seconds later, we tumbled down the crooked back stairs into the kitchen. There, Huntly's mother stood, brown hair softening her weary face. She hugged a loose cardigan close to her thin chest. Somehow, she lacked my mother's vitality. She looked sad and worn down. I spotted lines on her forehead and by her thin lips. The little crinkle lines that form from laughing were not there. She was absent a generous swipe of lipstick to greet her public in the bookshop. Nothing like Mom, I noted. Then, she emitted a long sigh.

As I claimed a cookie, I wondered why neither Huntly, nor her mother, ever mentioned Huntly's father. He was like one of the ghosts from colonial times that Huntly and I pictured haunting this house. Once, I heard a door slam upstairs followed by a loud exclamation, "Damn!" I knew that was no ghost. When I glanced at my friend, she was staring up at the ceiling. She avoided my look. Her mother was gripping the edge of the deep ceramic sink, exhaling loudly. My heart tripped over itself. My

Dad said *damn, shit,* and *Jeeezus Chreeest* sometimes, but no one ever gripped a piece of furniture when he did. Sometimes, we giggled. After what had felt like a long minute, Huntly's mother suggested we go outdoors to play. Right away.

Now, her mother said, "Finish your cheese sandwiches, girls. I must head back to the bookshop. If you promise to wash up thoroughly, I'll let you read a book." Was that where my life-long love affair with reading deepened to passion? Curled up in a window-seat in that impressive bookshop, I might listen to raindrops pattering against the blurry glass panes, tucked on velvet pillows behind books, books, and even more books. What a stark contrast to the cold marble floors and towering white statues of old men in togas inside the Beverly Public Library. There, librarians shushed me when my voice rose above a whisper. Leaning forward, I let my fingers skip toward the conclusion of *The Wind in the Willows* story. Such heaven, sniffing the leather-bound volumes of the *Encyclopedia Britannica* one aisle away from my personal perch, gladdening when the strong friendship between Mole, Rat, Badger, and Toad prevailed against their enemies. Huntly and I never tired of this story with its imaginative illustrations.

On sunnier days, we had exclusive access to the thick woods behind the Hale Farm and Bookshop. That chain link fence on the Bancroft Circle side prevented entry from the general public. Inside our world, centuries-old beech trees with gnarled trunks made their tenacious way skyward. These ancient trees were Huntly's and my companions. One of us would scramble up a trunk, gaining a solid toehold with our canvas sneakers. Then, an arm would reach down to hoist up the other. Swinging side by side on a rough branch, we'd spin stories about the earliest family of Hales. Had they hidden messages in the mossy crevasses? Or tucked away small treasures? We never did find an elusive parchment note rolled up, hidden in a hole. We so hoped for a scribbled message from the dead. Perhaps a seventeenth-century girl our age had scrawled out a plea for help. "Save me! They say I am bewitched!" Or perhaps the Reverend Hale's wife had penned a short note saying she feared being hung for simply being the target of ignorant gossips. We weren't sure how we'd rescue these girls and women given the passage of more than 250 years. We just knew that we were eager to help. Alas, the only paper messages we retrieved were our own, soggy and barely recognizable, thanks to Mother Nature.

Sitting among the dense trees, we could not make out any Bancroft Circle homes around us. This space was our personal park. The protective canopy of beeches and chestnuts gave us complete privacy. Huntly, an only child, had a proprietary sense of the sanctuary. "It belongs to me," she said. "Of course, I am willing to share with you, Kristin."

From our perch, we'd get dizzy gazing up at the blue tableau filled with puffy white clouds. "Straight up! See, it's an elephant." A few minutes later, I'd pipe up. "It's moving, becoming a cat." The sun, peeking behind the elephant-now-cat cloud, made us shield our eyes with our hands. Warmer days were coming. Summer! After that, hooray, first grade. On that noteworthy morning, we'd meet at the corner of Hale and Dane to be escorted safely across the busy street to the gravel commons and grass around Hardie School. But this breezy April afternoon, September felt as far away as the moon.

I repositioned my fanny into a more comfortable groove offered by this tree. The temperature was dropping enough to prompt me to button my sweater to my chin. Huntly stood, squeezing past me to the empty branch on the opposite side.

Brushing off her musty fingers, she used the trunk for a backrest. We were mirror images of each other, perfectly in sync, I realized. Huntly was my height and weight. We both had shoulder-length straight hair, although mine was dark brown. When I smiled, she followed suit. We took our cues from each other. My sister Joan, my so-called Irish twin, would always be a grade ahead of me, always protect me. More often than not, I took my cues from her. But Huntly and I were co-equals. We'd be in the same grade up to and including Beverly High School. Together, forever. We had already pledged that she'd be in my wedding, and I'd be in hers. Little did we know that those events would never come to pass.

Huntly retrieved two cookies from her jacket pocket, tossing one to me. "Good catch," she said. "I stole them when Mom wasn't looking." We munched in companionable silence. Time-worn trees stretched up, up, and away. A breeze knocked the thinner limbs against one another, creating a clacking noise. Huntly said, "Hey, they sound like old people, whose false teeth don't fit into their mouths." We chuckled, confident that we'd never be like that.

Then, she cleared her throat. "Guess what? I learned something wonderful today. I've been bursting to tell you."

I rearranged my body for more extended branch sitting. "So, tell me!"

"Mom and I were talking this morning about my fifth birthday party even if it's not until late June. That's when she told me that I am old enough to know how special I am. Because . . . I'm adopted." She gave a loud whoop.

I fidgeted, playing with a button on my sweater. "But what does that mean?"

I had never known anyone who was adopted. I had not read about it. Mom and Dad had not told me about it. My older sisters and my brother had not confided in me either. If they had a clue about what adoption meant, I was sure they would have flaunted it, just as they had last December when they revealed that there was no Santa Claus.

"Kristin, everyone but you knows there is no Santa Claus!" Similarly, they would have taunted me by saying, "You might be the adopted one. Who knows?" Were I adopted, I was sure, they would have delighted in being the spoilers in informing me about our family secret.

Huntly peeked her head around the trunk. She pinched my arm. "Here's how it works. Most kids are born into a family. Like you. Your parents can make babies. But some can't. So, if they want a kid, they go to a place where there are lots of babies to choose from. My mom and dad looked at all of them—and chose me! Adopted kids are special because we get picked."

She clapped her hands, her face pink with pleasure. "Now you know my secret. No secrets between us. Not now, not ever. That's what we promised when we pricked our fingers and mixed our blood," she reminded me. As if I needed the reminder.

We sat, cradled by the limbs of this centuries-old tree. It had survived the American Revolution, the Civil War, and two World Wars. It was the perfect repository for Huntly's amazing revelation.

By now, the sun was dropping in the sky. Playtime was over. Huntly stood, carefully embracing the trunk. She looked down at the ground.

"One, two, three, jump!" she yelled. We landed on our feet, knees bracing on impact. We hugged each other, a little tighter than usual. "See you!" She raced back toward the Hale Farm.

I watched as her figure got smaller and smaller until she reached the kitchen door. Then, I heard it slam. I stood, absorbing this news as she was swept up into the dark interior of the Hale House.

I made a beeline for my backyard, also slamming our kitchen door behind me. Per usual, Mom was in her starched apron, preoccupied with dinner. She brushed her hair from her forehead as her fingers pressed down against the red worn spine of *The Fanny Farmer Cookbook*. I breathed in the wonderful aroma of meatloaf baking in the oven. Despite the cookies and the lunch, my stomach was growling.

"Your sister Joan already set the dining room table. You owe her a favor for that."

Mom fiddled with knobs on the electric stove, talking her checklist out loud. "Biscuits and potatoes in the oven with the meatloaf, green beans ready to boil. Enough time to relax over an Old Fashioned with Dad," she said, turning to face me, hands on hips. She knelt to be in my line of vision. I saw how her eyes lit up and her smile widened after mentioning my father. She put her warm palms over my cheeks. "You, my pet, must have been outdoors a good long time. How was your day? You sound out of breath."

"Yes, I am." I was filled with pent-up energy and important news. Huntly had not made me promise not to share her secret with my parents. I had a hunch that I wasn't to blab it to friends but was less sure about my siblings. "Mom, Huntly told me that she is special because she's adopted. Is she more special than me?"

Mom embraced me. She tweaked one of my short brown pigtails.

43

"Honey, you are special. As are Joan, Bud, and Susan. No one in this family is adopted because your father and I had children easily, goodness knows. We had one after another within four and a half years, top to bottom. Each of you is special and an important part of our family. We love you all equally. But some parents who want babies keep trying without luck. That's when they adopt. Huntly is special because she was selected by her mother and father to make them a family."

My nose, buried in Mom's soft hair, inhaled her Breck shampoo. I caught a faint whiff of her Chanel No. 5 cologne. Then I sniffed the scent of homemade bread, a delicious combination. All these smells I associated with Mom. And with love. No longer was I holding my breath.

Mom whispered, "We had no need to adopt. If we had, we would have picked you, for sure." She kissed my flushed cheek before releasing me.

Less than two months later, on a warm June morning, my world changed dramatically. When Huntly didn't call, I called her. After all, it would soon be her birthday. But there was no response, only a recording saying the number was no longer in service. Next, I dashed over to Hale Farm and rang the bell. Over and over. I walked around the house, peeking in the downstairs windows. No one in the kitchen. No dirty dishes in the sink. No sign of life.

And that's when I noticed Mr. Puggles. He was lying on his side by the back door. Huntly adored that stuffed dog. She'd never leave him behind, would she? I held back a sob. Huntly had to have been upset when she learned he was missing. What had distracted her, kept her from safeguarding him? A witch? A ghost from the past? Or a ghost from the present?

44

As far as I was concerned, it might as well have been witch-craft, my best friend disappearing without a trace. When I pestered Mom and Dad, they shook their heads, as puzzled as I was.

The book shop closed. Huntly's father's co-workers at Metal Hydrides in Beverly said he was still showing up at work. But he was not volunteering the whereabouts of his wife and daughter.

One summer day, I spotted Mom chatting over the hedge with Esther, who was gesturing in the direction of the Hale Farm. When I ran outside to meet Mom, she ushered me home.

"Honey, please, sit. I will tell you what Esther told me about what happened that June night when Huntly and her mother vanished." I sat, trembling, my hands folded in my lap.

According to Esther, my mother explained, the marriage had been troubled because of Newt's drinking problems. Martha absconded with Huntly, with Esther's help, fleeing to the opposite side of the country where he could not trace them.

Of course, I asked Mom where that might be. She shook her head, shrugged her shoulders. She bent down to put her face opposite mine and put a finger to her lips. "That's as much as I know, my love." She was vague, purposefully so. In hind-sight, I realize it was her way of keeping Martha and Huntly safe. "As a dear friend to Huntly, I'm confident you can keep this big secret."

California, Oregon, and Washington in the early 1950s might as well have been Siberia. An avid map reader, I dug out a Rand McNally atlas, running my finger slowly across the entire width of the United States before tracing it up and down the Pacific coast from Canada to Mexico, holding back tears.

Why, I wondered, did I never get a letter from my friend? If she had sent it to Kristin Elliott Christmas Cards, Dad would have picked it up in PO Box 23. But he never did. During first grade, I'd examine the mail that flopped through the metal slot in the front door onto our Dane Street wooden hall floor. No post mark from California, Oregon, or Washington; no envelope with Huntly's handwriting. Eventually, I gave up my futile quest.

It would be many decades before I'd learn the whole truth, from Huntly herself. She'd become an investigative reporter. With her formidable research skills, she was in search of her biological parents. She'd sought help with childhood memories. Her innate curiosity had led to me. How fascinating to still recognize each other after a seventy-one-year hiatus! Over a long lunch, filled with laughter and tears, she revealed that she had an adopted daughter.

Huntly filled in many of the blanks for me about that frightening midnight escape her mother had planned to protect the two of them. Indeed, her father had been abusive and an alcoholic, a disease rarely acknowledged in 1950. Her mother had awakened her from a deep sleep and swept her, the stuffed dog, and one suitcase out of the house, tiptoeing over to Esther's. Somehow, by the time they had reached Boston's South Station to catch a train headed to the West Coast, Huntly had discovered Mr. Puggles was missing. She said, "I was inconsolable, crying a lot." She added that her mother was persuaded to cut all ties with Beverly in case her husband decided to come after them. "Sheer terror was behind our eerie silence," she said.

Without this half-a-century-later knowledge, my four-year-old mind had conjured up a story that my friend's fate had something to do with sorcery. One day she was present, the next day, presto! Abracadabra! Poof! Gone. Wasn't that how magic worked? Witchcraft and mystery went hand in hand with the Hale Farm. Some of it must have rubbed off on its subsequent—and most recent—inhabitants.

Throughout childhood, when walking over to the wooded area in Bancroft Circle behind the Hale House, I would circle the cold chain links of the Bancroft Circle barrier with my index finger. Always uninviting. No longer could I gain entrance into our wooded sanctuary. I'd press my face against the metal fence. If I stared hard enough, was that Huntly, waving to me from the lowest branch of the beech tree?

JEEPERS CREEPERS

THE LYRICS from this 1930s song crooned by the likes of Louis Armstrong and Frank Sinatra immediately bring back memories of two simmering summers from my childhood. At age six, heat meant putting on a bathing suit and heading for a local beach. The seconds it took me to strip off my shorts and shirt in exchange for a swimsuit were full of anticipation. Soon, I'd be building sandcastles, digging a deep moat, then diving into the waves and floating on my back in the brisk salt water.

One day in the late summer of 1951 turned out to be more than a carefree beach excursion. In the kitchen, my father encircled all four of us kids within his long arms and let us know that he'd need our cooperation, as he was about to leave on a temporary assignment with his former employer, Sylvania Electric. "Kristin Elliott Cards needs a little boost," he said.

Looking up at Dad's face in the kitchen, I could see above his strained smile, a frown creasing his forehead.

Feeling his soft kiss on my cheek, I wondered if Dad had ever been gone overnight? Though openly demonstrative with Mom, it was unusual for him to show us affection like this.

"I know you'll be good and mind your mother," he said. "I'll be back before you miss me. Bud, you're the man of the house. Got it?" Bud puffed with pride. I decided if Dad was okay with my brother being the man of the house, I would be, too. Then, hearing a car engine idling in our driveway, Dad rose up tall from his squat and strode to the front door.

At the threshold, Mom stood on tiptoe to brush a wavy lock of black hair from his eyes. They wrapped their arms around each other, his thin five-feet eleven-inch frame towering over her five-feet two-inch slim figure. Their long hug and kiss revealed their mutual displeasure at being separated. She whispered, "You'll be bringing home good money, just what the business needs." Another quick kiss. He grabbed his plaid cotton suitcase, straightened his tie, and slipped out the front door.

Susan, Bud, Joan, and I followed him. Standing on the front stoop, we must have looked like the longest angle of a triangle given our top-to-bottom heights: Susan, eleven; Bud, nine; Joan, seven; and me, six. Dad hopped into a Ford sedan next to his boss, who was driving, and rewarded our good-byes with a generous wave. Standing behind Bud, Mom reached for his shoulder and gave it a squeeze.

"Isn't it lucky Dad's colleagues value him so much?" Mom said. I wasn't feeling lucky now though, just sad. Mom went on to explain how Dad's engineering skills were still prized by his Sylvania colleagues. And how his boss had been understanding when Dad had turned down the relocation offer to Pennsylvania. She underlined that his supervisor thought it was great that my father was starting a family business. "Such a nice man! To give Kristin Elliott Christmas Cards the shot in the arm it needs!" She signed. "Even so, it's rough when Dad has to travel for work."

Mom pivoted to let us scooch under her arm before we went back inside. "Let's look on the bright side. We've been left with the station wagon," she said. Finally, I spotted her smile. The night before, we'd heard the middle-aged weatherman on our new black and white Westinghouse television set promise another day of hot and humid August weather, the kind Dad labelled "dog days of summer." The forecast? A perfect excuse to load the car for West Beach. It was only five miles up the Beverly coast. We loved cooling off in the ocean as much as Brandy, our beloved wire-haired Fox Terrier. We clapped our hands. "West Beach!" We anticipated every part of it, the clubhouse that sold popsicles, the long stretches of sand, the gentle waves, and the long wooden pier with its high and low diving boards. Our fingers would wrinkle like raisins before Mom could persuade us to come out of the water and back on land.

We knew the West Beach drill by heart. Mom pulled out cotton beach towels; bathing caps; the plaid woolen family blanket; a plastic, striped folding beach chair; and a straw basket filled with homemade sandwiches, deviled eggs, and a thermos of lemonade. At the last minute, she tossed in a leash for Brandy, who never strayed from food and family long enough to require it. Brandy cocked her wiry head and vigorously wagged her stubby tail. Chasing waves and fetching ball with two-legged family people? These activities were her terrier idea of a perfect day. And ours too.

Several hours later, when we reached home, we spilled out of the station wagon with sticky limbs and sand lodged in our damp suits. It also got into our canvas Keds sneakers, donned at the beach, because otherwise, the sand scorched our feet. Our sunburned skin felt scratchy from the saltwater.

To get rid of the first layer of sand before going indoors, it was our habit to spray ourselves with the garden hose. Brandy's mouth opened, eager to drink in water and play with the spray. We took turns before handing over the hose to the next sibling who'd gain access to the shower upstairs. That day, Mom must have been entering orders for the business or starting dinner. We heard her singing "Jeepers Creepers," the part about someone with strange, large eyes. At one point, she called out, "Kristin, don't forget to turn on the floor fan in the upstairs hall. I don't think your sisters or brother bothered to do it."

Despite the shades that were pulled down, the house felt like a steamy jungle. As I trudged upstairs, the air seemed more oppressive. No ocean breeze to relieve the heat that threw out blasts as much as a furnace. The shades made no soft *flap, flap* against screens. They were as limp as we were, as we listlessly wiped away the residue of the beach. No birds chirped in the tree outside the upstairs bedroom that I shared with Joan. The fierce yellow ball of fire in the sky would throw down more heat well after its setting.

Suddenly, amidst the heavy air, there was a piercing scream.

It was Mom. A scream unlike any I'd ever heard. It came from directly below. Joan and I fled from our bedroom, down the hall, and collided with Susan as she headed for the stairs. Brandy yipped. We stopped short of tripping over the fan as its blades swiveled unsuccessfully to move the thick air. Bud emerged from the bathroom with a towel wrapped around his dripping torso. He wedged in front of our posse and led the charge.

In the kitchen, Mom was by the back door, wielding a cast iron frying pan in her right hand, swinging it in the air like a saber. "How dare he!" she shouted.

"Who?". . . "What?" We talked on top of each other, shivering, despite the heat. The kitchen fan failed its mission to cool our flushed skin. The blades clicked and clacked over our mother's erratic breathing.

Mom tossed her head back. Still clutching the frying pan, she said, "It happened so suddenly. One minute, I was patting flour for the fried chicken. The next, I heard a creak on the back porch and a scratch on the screen door. I knew Brandy was upstairs with you, so it wasn't the dog asking to be let in."

I stared at her as she recounted what happened and how scared she'd been. This was a kitchen utensil-wielding, armed mother standing her ground, a mother I'd never witnessed before. Her eyes were flashing. Her fist still clenched the heavy pan. Mom continued, "I twirled around, and there he was with his hand shielding his eyes from the sun. He started to come in. That's when I let it rip. Thank God, he retreated into the vacant lot. Did any of you see or hear anything?"

We shook our heads in unison. The shades were all the way down, the way we kept them in August, I wanted to remind her. But I kept my mouth shut. In my imagination, the Hardy Boys or even Nancy Drew would have spotted several clues already. How did we come up short?

Mom finally put down the black cast iron pan. She squeezed her hands before wrapping her arms around her aproned waist. "I'm going to call the police. I doubt there is much they can do. Meanwhile, go finish showering and get dressed. They may want to ask you questions." Her face remained pink. The hand that had held her weapon was still shaking when she picked up the black receiver to call the precinct.

Brrring! Brrring! A few minutes later, the piercing doorbell announced the police officers' arrival.

"Mrs. Charles Elliott?" asked the middle-aged, uniformed man, who doffed his hat to reveal a moist bald head. Sweat slowly trickled down his forehead. Behind him, his partner shifted his stance.

Bud reached the door before Mom. "My mother is here—behind me, sir."

Dad had instructed us to address authority figures in uniform by their titles. "Be respectful," he advised. Dad also said that the cop who wore the badge and carried the gun represented authority and law and order. After all, his father had been a cop. Right now, Dad would have been proud of Bud.

Mom gestured for them to sit at the Formica kitchen table. The officer who'd shadowed his superior pulled out a small notepad, jotting comments down. *Clack, clack* . . . the blades of the fan kept up their valiant battle. I stared at the cops' navy-blue uniforms. Woolen! Just like those of the junior and senior high school bands. We all felt sorry for them when they marched miles down Cabot and Hale Streets in the Memorial Day weekend parade.

Ever the hostess, Mom asked if they'd like homemade iced tea or lemonade. Gratefully, they accepted. As she popped ice cubes from a tray and poured tall glasses from the pitcher, Brandy's little claws pattered against the shiny linoleum floor. They clicked as the fan clacked. She plopped down next to Mom's feet, keeping a watchful eye on the two strangers. Dad would have been proud of her, too.

53

The two officers gulped their drinks, wiping their mouths on the sleeves of their jackets. Together, they agreed to pace out the perimeter of our house and back yard, and to spend a few minutes in the empty back lot.

When they came back, they looked more parched, and swiped at the weeds and twigs that clung to their trousers. Without prompting, Mom refilled their glasses.

"Look, ma'am, we couldn't see hide nor hair of anyone," the bald officer said. "Whoever he is, rest assured that he's harmless, a Peeping Tom. He sneaks a peek under the window shade. Sees a woman, all by her lonesome. No hubby, no kids. No doubt he's scared of his own shadow. No breaking and entering here. He gets his jollies slinking around, peeping. Ha, ha, that's how he gets his nickname. You did a good job frightening him, young lady," he said. "Waving that cast iron pan was just the thing."

His fellow officer chuckled. "In our opinion, he won't return."

The bald officer swiped his face with a hanky retrieved from his pants back pocket. It was limp from repeated use. "Nothing else to do here. If you want my advice? With a husband on the road, little lady, you've gotta lock the doors and windows. Good luck on a day in the nineties like today. Not what you want to hear during this August heat wave, but what a pretty lady must do."

Mom's face did not hide a frown. This back-and-forth conversation between her and these two men was nothing like the flirting I'd witnessed with the tradesmen who delivered our milk and fish. I became aware of a tap, tap, tapping. Her fingers were angrily making their own music against the kitchen counter.

"Here's my theory, officers," she said. "This stranger may have been casing our neighborhood, maybe even spying on us. He noticed Charlie leave with a valise this morning. Late this afternoon, he saw me pull our station wagon into the driveway. He waited, until sure that I was alone in the kitchen. Then, he made his move. I don't agree that approaching me via the back door is what you call a Peeping Tom episode. He pushed the screen door open. Only my scream, plus the pan in his face, made him beat a retreat."

The bald cop said, "Hmmm. That's your theory, miss. But our report must deal with the evidence. We'll fill in the episode as a Peeping Tom. Nothing more law enforcement can do. For sure, we don't have the resources for a stakeout. No, siree! For what it's worth, your husband might reconsider leaving you alone with the kids."

He donned his hat. "Thanks for the lemonade." The second cop scrambled to his feet.

Bud ushered the duo to the front door, glaring at their backs as they walked down the steps and into the black police car. Mom said, "I've always been fond of this cast iron frying pan, now more than ever. I'm going to fry up the best chicken breasts and legs ever. I've already prepared a yummy potato salad. Who's the hungriest?" All hands shot up. "Your father will be proud of you. He'll also have something to say about all of this."

They talked quietly that evening on the phone, long after we kids had gone to bed. I strained to listen from my twin bed at the end of the upstairs hall, but unsuccessfully.

The stranger did not return. However, Mom and Dad's embrace two days later set a record for time and intensity. He gently cupped her cheeks as he kissed her. Then he dropped his tall frame to his knees, gathering us in a group hug.

How unlike his normal reserved self, I thought.

"I don't like a cop telling your mother what we should or should not do. Even so, for the immediate future, I'm not taking any chances. No overnights with Sylvania. The hell with Peeping Toms." It was Dad's understated way of saying we were too precious to chance fate.

To the best of my recollection, he never accepted another overnight assignment with Sylvania. Chance, or fate? A deus ex machina swooped down in the form of Mom's Uncle Hubert. He had died, generously leaving my mother $5,000, a bonanza in the early 1950s. That generous gift was just the infusion that the wobbly Kristin Elliott Christmas Card business needed to survive beyond its infancy.

As for the Peeping Tom? He never peeped around our neighborhood again. Sadly, another creepy event took us by surprise. Only it was me, not my mother, who was the target.

It was a year later and another dog day in August. Mom had encouraged Dad to play golf with friends, something he almost never did. We kids lined up expectantly next to the station wagon for West Beach. Bud's best friend Evan, a close neighbor, had walked over from his Bancroft Circle house. On the way home, we wheedled Mom to open the tailgate, and to take the back road in the woods so she could accelerate at the Slippery Rock bump, a sudden incline that felt like a rollercoaster to us. *Thump!* Our heads banged against the interior roof as Bud and Evan pantomimed falling out of the rear of the station wagon. We whooped and hollered, delighted by the smack against our fannies. Predictably, Mom put her index finger to her lips: our little secret.

Minutes later, Mom pulled into the driveway, shifting into park. Evan and Bud peeled out, racing toward Evan's house.

"Home before dinner," Mom admonished. Bud's hand shot up in acknowledgement, his damp bathing suit flapping against his lean limbs.

Susan, Joan, and I headed for the back yard, Brandy yipping. We started our splashing in the hose game. Then suddenly, Susan remembered she'd forgotten to buy a friend's birthday present for a party. Like the captain of the boat, she commanded her crew—Joan and me—that she'd shower first. She asked Mom to drive her downtown to Webber's Department Store before it closed, and slapped the hose into Joan's hands. Her turn to rinse the sand out from between her toes and the nooks and crannies inside her bathing suit, sewn by our mom. Susan yelled from the upstairs bathroom window, "All yours, Joan. Back in a few."

At last, my turn. Happily, Brandy enjoyed my company. I suspected that she favored me over my older siblings because I took extra time to pick her up and rub her soft ears, sniffing her clean dog scent. Of course, she was interested in hearing about my day.

"Don't use all the hot water," I shouted to the upstairs empty window.

Joan's head appeared in shadow at the screen. "I will give you fair warning."

Less than five minutes later, I heard, "All yours, little sister. There might even be some hot water left. Ha, ha!"

I skipped through the kitchen, feeling the lack of Mom's presence. This was her kingdom, where she ruled supreme. Here, she moved pots and pans effortlessly from drawers to stovetop to the oven. There was a hint of Chanel No. 5. But mostly, the room gave off pleasant whiffs of our upcoming meal: macaroni and cheese, and brownies. Mom was like

Houdini, working her magic, in control of her props. We were her appreciative audience.

Taking the stairs two at a time, my small hand grabbed the banister to help thrust me up. I couldn't wait to stick my head under the shower and get out the grains of sand stuck in my bellybutton, even if I'd drawn the last straw for shower privileges. While I pulled off my bathing suit in our bedroom, Joan edged past me. "Hang that in the tub while you shower. Take as long as you like. Meanwhile, I'll be downstairs reading *The Secret of the Old Clock*."

"Hey, that's our Nancy Drew," I reminded her. She shrugged. It was our ongoing book-sharing war. Once I got dressed and down to the living room, I'd find her sitting cross-legged in the wing chair, engrossed in the plot that I longed to devour.

I remembered that tune made famous by Louis Armstrong that had been playing on the radio in the car, this time a Bing Crosby rendition, more upbeat, which made the lyrics about weeping eyes as weapons seem odd. I didn't know then that "Jeepers Creepers" was a reference to Jesus Christ. But the tune stuck in my brain.

I kept humming it while laying out shorts, a seersucker blouse, cotton underpants, and an undershirt to change into. Then, completely naked, I opened the bedroom door. My eyes took in the length of the hall, beyond Mom and Dad's bedroom to my right, and the door to Sue and Bud's bedroom opposite the bathroom.

At the top of the stairs on the landing stood the overweight, thirteen-year-old boy who lived next door. He always kept to himself, played with no one. What was he doing? I stared. He stared back. His face glistened. Mostly, I noticed that he was smiling, but his grin didn't look natural. His tongue was darting back and forth, licking his slimy lips, like a snake anticipating his prey. Nothing shielded my nude body from his predatory glare. Then, he stepped toward me.

I screamed bloody murder and ran backwards, slamming my bedroom door shut. Then, I propelled myself into the rear of the closet, diving behind hangers and clothes, but not before closing the door with my foot. Instinctively, I pushed my hand into my mouth to silence the sound of my whimpering. The only sound I heard while rocking back and forth was my heartbeat *thump, thump, thumping* hard against my bare, flat chest. It hurt. And it was too loud. What felt like minutes later, the closet handle began to turn. I heard the click as if it were a death sentence. My heart seemed to stop. I froze.

"Kristin, are you in there?" It was Joan. "He's gone. Come out. You're safe." I took my fist from my mouth and saw how my sharp teeth had made a nasty red impression on my palm. Joan's hand plunged through the hangers and clothes, pulling me up. Helping me out. Letting me know I was safe.

She hugged me as I sobbed.

"After your scream, I raced up the stairs. He slammed me aside as he fled out the front door. Don't worry, Mom will take care of this. Get dressed now. I'll even loan you the Nancy Drew. Okay?"

As we stumbled from the closet, Joan cocked her head. "Hey, I hear Mom pulling into the driveway now. We'll tell her what happened together."

I wiped away my tears. My heartbeat was slowing. Joan pulled me closer. She smelled like Dial soap. I guessed that this creepy boy would have smelled gross, like a dead frog, and that he had foul breath, too. I was relieved I did not know for certain.

People talked little about mental illness in the early 1950s. The next day, Mom marched next door to talk with his parents. His mother confided that her teenaged son was awaiting acceptance to a special needs boarding school run by a Catholic order. She had hopes that he would enter the priesthood one day. Following their conversation, the neighbors expedited his application.

After this terrifying episode, the troubled neighborhood boy never bothered me again. My scream had scared him away. But he wasn't just another Peeping Tom. He had dared to come into our house, to stalk the most vulnerable Elliott. Me.

And he chose his moment when neither parent was around. Even Susan and Bud were gone. Had the same two cops dropped by, they probably wouldn't have done anything. After all, they might say, no property was damaged. No one was injured or hurt. Nothing was taken.

I disagree. This Peeping Tom got a long look at my starkly naked body. I'd been scared out of my wits. The incident felt like a huge violation. Something shattered inside me during our staring contest. It took me a long time to put it together. And to put it behind me. I knew for certain I'd never want to hear that "Jeepers Creepers" song again.

THE GRANDMOTHER WE FEARED

WAS I FOUR YEARS OLD when my family visited Grandpa Elliott in a Waltham hospital following his stroke? Dad's father was an easy-going, handsome man with a shock of white hair and twinkly blue eyes. Even propped up against several starched pillows, in blue flannel pajamas, he sat erect and appeared tall, maybe even taller than my father. He spread both hands over the thin woolen blankets, inviting us grandkids to hop up on the bed. Like a magician, Grandpa would turn his calloused hands over to palms that were hiding hard candy balls, two in the left palm, two in the right. We children gathered by his bedside, exclaiming with delight.

Suddenly, there was a shadow. To waylay us, Grandma Elliott had lurched from her chair. She was stern, dressed in black, with a deformed foot stabilized by a metal brace. Was she going to snatch away our candies? Her brace hit the metal hospital bed frame. *Clang! Clang!*

She had anticipated our small stampede. "Now, William. How you spoil them. They shouldn't eat treats between meals." He winked at us, passed us the candy, yet did not contradict her.

"Your grandfather needs rest," she said. "Peace and quiet. You little ones go down the hall and entertain yourselves. Close the door behind you on your way out." As she chided, she pointed at the door as if we didn't remember how we'd entered. We glanced at our parents, who nodded. We had our marching orders. Candy in fists, we hightailed it away from the grownups. Even at such a young age, I could not fathom how such a dour woman had won the heart of my gentle grandfather. He was so unlike her.

Later, in the stuffy waiting room, Mom and Dad stood over us, signaling the end of the visit. Luckily, Susan had grabbed a deck of cards on the way out of our house so we could play Crazy Eights.

On the drive home to Beverly, we peppered Dad and Mom with questions. How had our father's parents met? How did a good-looking man end up with a witch? Dad winced when we used that word. But he didn't correct us. We wanted to know if she hated us since she was always shooing us away.

"How much older than Grandpa is Grandma Elliott?" Joan asked from the prized middle seat in the front of the car. We kids coveted it and took turns rotating seats on our road trips. Dad kept his eyes on the steady stream of traffic on Route 128. Joan added, "She looks much older. Even though he's the one in the hospital."

Dad chuckled. "Not much older, only four years. She's had a tough life. Leaving Ireland and relocating to a new country at the turn of the century took guts. And knowing she'd have to send money home to County Roscommon to bring other relatives to America. What's more, being born with a deformed foot was a serious liability for a young woman. She must have said a silent Hail Mary the day she set eyes on my father, standing erect in his Boston City Police uniform."

Dad continued, "I can only hazard a guess as to why he was taken with her. Not for her beauty. Maybe her brains? She's a helluva strong person. She overcame being an Irish immigrant, having a physical deformity, and being a stranger in a strange land. My father isn't ambitious. But he is kind and compassionate. I'm guessing he instinctively realized that she had enough get-up-and-go for the two of them. Once she decides to do something, get out of her way!"

Mom piped up from the front, "She might have been as surprised as everyone else when he proposed. Lots of younger women set their cap for him. Despite the competition, she would not give an inch on religion."

We back-seaters leaned forward to chime in. Susan, Bud, and I sat up straight to hear better.

"What do you mean?" Susan asked.

Dad cleared his throat, eyes on the highway. "She made my Protestant father agree to bring us up in the Roman Catholic religion." We had heard bits and pieces of this story before, but never in one fell swoop. Dad mentioned how his father understood how central the church was to her sense of self, so he didn't resist her request. I twisted the piping on the front seat cover, knowing that my father didn't care about God, the Son, or the Holy Ghost.

Dad said, "My father caved. As your Uncle Los and I became young men, Mother demanded we raise our children in the church. We agreed, also taking the path of least resistance." Dad sighed. "Growing up Catholic was, for me, growing up in fear of God, the Pope, the archbishops, the priests, the nuns. Then there was confession and communion. It made me want to vomit. Why would I make you kids go through that?"

Dad held one hand off the wheel, pointing toward the dashboard, directing our attention. "And you know what? My older brother Lawrence and I both made her the same promise. And, later, we both broke it."

Front-seaters and back-seaters were silent for a stretch of road. Dad seemed relieved to have told us why we were not Catholics. I felt relieved that I did not have to offer up a juicy confession every week to a priest sitting behind a dusty muslin curtain.

Mom picked up the story thread. "Dad and I eloped. For your grandmother's sake, we remarried a few days later in the Catholic Church. Appeasing her by agreeing to raise you Catholic is a lie I'll always regret." She picked at a hangnail on her hand. I angled myself from the raised portion of the middle of the back seat—the dreaded hump—to catch my father's reflection in the rear-view mirror.

He grabbed the wheel with both hands again, and not because a truck or car had cut in front of us. His jaw clenched. "Well, Betsy, that's water over the dam. We thought we were doing her a kindness. She was happy telling her parish priest that all her grandchildren were keeping the faith. We did tell her the truth eventually. It was too hard maintaining the lie."

Joan put her hand on Dad's arm. "That's why we've never stepped foot in a Catholic church!"

"Exactly. That's my point. The Mother Church has a saying: Give me a child until he's five, and he's mine for life. To this day,

I remember my mother in her long black dress dragging me to Mass to show me off to the congregation in my velveteen jacket and white shirt with lace trimming. I looked like Little Lord Fauntleroy." He laughed but it wasn't a happy belly laugh. More like a groan from deep within.

Bud scowled and said, "Yuck!"

I asked, "Is being Catholic bad?" We'd be home shortly, as we had just exited off the Route 128 ramp in Beverly. The acrid smells wafting from our town dump at this intersection always assaulted my nostrils. I knew we were only three miles from Dane Street, but I was greedy to hear more.

"Not bad, Kristin. More like . . . upsetting. It sounds petty, but we had little money so my mother bought the smelliest, cheapest kinds of fish. To this day, the only fish I can tolerate is well-disguised, like fried clams. There were times when I invented a venal sin to satisfy the bored priest on the other side of the confessional. The smell of incense still sticks in my craw. Walking into the church vestibule made my stomach churn. So much emphasis on sinning and dying. No way in hell was I going to expose you to that."

I sniffed the garbage burning, sending swirls of smoke in the air. Dad was winding down. He said, "I feel guilty that my older brother bears the brunt of caring for our parents. He lives a few miles away so he can stop by more frequently. Still, at least we pitch in with support money, which he can't, given that he's living on a schoolteacher's pay."

Almost home now, Mom chimed in, "Even with Los' unfailing willingness to do your grandmother's bidding, Dad is still her favorite son. Her younger boy was always the one she spoiled." Mom reached over Joan to give Dad's shoulder a little squeeze.

Mom's gesture cut off the pained look on Dad's face. He was frowning, no doubt remembering that Lord Fauntleroy outfit.

Everyone fell silent again, absorbing this history. We never had smelly fish, only the freshest that was delivered in person by Sam, the fishmonger. Dad would treat us once in a while to fried clams and French fries from the HoJo's in North Beverly. I had no idea what incense smelled like, but my father rated it up there with gross fish. As for squeezing into a confessional to share my secret sins with a priest? That felt scary.

Perched between Mom and Dad, Joan leaned her head on Mom's shoulder. Mom patted the top of her head. I felt sad for Dad. And glad for us. Thank goodness, he had given us this gift of freedom. Of thinking for ourselves. If not, I would have only one more year in the Catholic religion before the church owned me for life!

Not long after this visit, Grandpa Elliott died. After that, when we visited Waltham, we went to an apartment in a building dedicated to elderly women affiliated with my grandmother's church.

We'd climb into the station wagon for the hour-long drive. Mom would say, "Your mother loves having you to herself, Charlie. Such a shame she has so little patience with her grandchildren. Well, with the slight exception of Susan." I was sitting next to my sister and felt her wince.

Mom continued, "Charlie, your mother will complain about how she sees so little of you. The sooner you tackle the to-do list, the better. Just ignore her criticism. The kids will fill her in on what they're up to. Mostly, she wants to talk our ears off telling us about church-related activities."

How we dreaded these trips, no one more than Dad. He'd push open the heavy front door of her building, a five-story

66

brick box that covered an entire block. Not a blade of grass, nor a Rose of Shannon bush, nor shrubs to soften the man-made edges. Dad shaded his eyes with one arm, peering through the dirty glass panel into the drab lobby. Once we got inside, we inhaled a whiff of greasy dinners prepared in tiny, airless kitchens. The electric bulb in the first-floor corridor cast as many shadows as light. The second-floor landing had an unresponsive switch that Dad kept flicking. "Add that to your list of chores," Mom muttered. Meanwhile, going upstairs, I'd been busy inventorying the framed pictures of Jesus: Jesus cradled in Mary's embrace; Jesus with his disciples at the Last Supper; Jesus at the crucifixion splayed on the cross. Grandma Elliott had a small crucifix affixed to her front door. Too many Jesuses by my grade-school math.

Dad whispered, "Did she not hear us clomping up the stairs?" He rapped sharply on her door, which was peeling with old paint. "Mother, we're here."

Scrape, scrape. Grandma Elliott's loopy stride preceded her as she yanked the door open.

She put her finger to her lips. "Shush! Let's not give the neighbors reason to complain." No kisses, only an awkward grasp to hug Dad. She was drowning in black, from the rustle of her below-the-knees rayon dress to the clunky, square-toed creased leather shoes. She'd long ago given up the attempt to create a waistline with her corset. She also had a musty old-lady odor that made my nose twitch. Clearly, she didn't dab cologne on the back of her wrists or behind her ears. Her thick stockings bunched around her ankles, whereas Mom's clear nylons revealed her shapely legs sliding into graceful heels. I'd never seen my mother in black. That day, she was wearing a turquoise shirtwaist that flowed from her narrow waist.

Thanks to a garish floral slipcover design, Grandma Elliott's wing chair stood out in the stuffy room. What an army of ugly purple flowers. Armrests and headrests defended fabric flowers with multiple lace antimacassars. Atop lacquered mahogany end tables, a contingent of white doilies assured no stains from moist glasses. These hand-stitched pieces were a united front in protecting every surface. They also testified to my grandmother's skill with her silent weapon, a crochet hook. Ultimately, they scolded us: *Do not think about staining wooden tables or upholstery with your sweaty bodies or sticky fingers!*

Mom held up a metal cookie tin and a meatloaf wrapped in aluminum foil. "Mother Elliott, I baked you a dinner, knowing how fond you are of meatloaf and brownies. I'll put the food in the fridge and leave the tin of brownies on your counter."

Grandma Elliott peered over her thick glasses, barely acknowledging her daughter-in-law. Her gray hair was pulled back in a severe bun. No makeup. I stared at a face filled with wrinkles. Maybe, like Mom said, a little application of lipstick could do no harm? Her cloudy eyes swept over Bud, Joan, and me, locking in on Susan. Wagging a gnarled index finger, she commanded, "Over here, young lady. I saved something for my smart granddaughter." Shuffling back to her wing chair, she reached for a small jewelry box. Dad glanced at Mom, who shrugged. Susan walked over cautiously, extending her small, smooth palm toward the arthritic one. As Grandma Elliott lifted the lid, Sue's face showed confusion. Inside lay a woman's gold watch, too clunky for a girl.

"It's made by the Waltham Watch Company, one of the best watch manufacturers in the country," our grandmother said. "The plant is only two miles from here. Isn't it pretty? It's gold plated yet looks genuine. Your late grandfather gave it to me. Now, it's yours."

Susan whispered, "Thank you," before snapping the lid shut, shoving it into her skirt pocket. Once home, she'd squirrel it away in the back of her bureau drawer along with other unwelcome Grandma Elliott gifts.

"How about a hug?" Grandma Elliott made a quick grab for my sister, who tolerated her tight grip for a second before worming free. "Children, help yourselves to a glass of water in the kitchen and one brownie each. But don't trail those crumbs in here. Charlie, here's my odd jobs list. Since you haven't been here in a long time, it's grown."

Now, traipsing into our grandmother's dark kitchen, we were happy Mom had brought her delicious brownies. Meanwhile, Dad had pulled a Hoover stand-up vacuum cleaner from a closet. After depositing our glasses in the sink and wiping our hands, we re-entered the living room to sit in a circle by my mother's and grandmother's feet. Already, Dad was on his hands and knees, scrubbing the cracked linoleum kitchen floor. Despite his elbow grease, the floors never looked spanking clean. Maybe it was the cracks in the flooring, or the permanent stains embedded in the beige carpet, which I bet the previous residents—most likely dead—had not noticed, due to failing vision. My grandmother, despite her ripening cataracts, saw dust, dirt, and grime everywhere.

We listened while Mom chatted about the family business. Grandma Elliott asked a few questions. Why was there never an interruption, a knock on her door? When we were at home, neighbors and friends came and went. Her telephone sat idle as a showpiece. Ours at home rang frequently. Only once, describing when the parish priest paid her a visit, did she reveal heaven-on-earth happiness. "He's so lovely, Father Kelly, making house calls, checking on us. Such a handsome boy. Reminds me of you, Charlie." Dad was wrapping up the vacuum cord. I saw him flinch.

Grandma Elliott said, "The young man thanked me for my faithful attendance at Mass." Her lips smacked. *Clatter, clatter!* Her false teeth, I guessed, giving me the heebie-jeebies.

Sunday afternoon visits pretty much followed this pattern. We also had a Christmas gift exchange that never deviated. After setting up a tabletop Christmas tree in her apartment, Dad drove home to Beverly with two lumpy wrapped packages. Inside each? Hand-made potholders. Mom would hold them up, poking her fingers through the too-generous loops. "Bigger than usual this year. All the better to burn my fingers." Mom and Dad laughed.

My grandmother outlived my grandfather by about five years. Along with my Uncle Los, Aunt Helen, and our cousins Judy and Don, we attended her funeral with Father Kelly officiating. Dad and Mom warned us that she had requested an open casket. They advised us not to glance down as we filed by. I was nine; Joan, ten; Bud, twelve; and Sue, fourteen. I swore to keep my eyes shut. At the last second, I could not resist. I snuck a peek.

Organ music was playing loudly in the background. Despite the pounding music chords, I overheard an old woman declare that she'd never seen Norah Hurley look better. My goodness, I thought, my grandmother's cheeks were rosy. Her lips were bright red! Someone had applied rouge, powder, and lipstick to her grey face. Her body seemed rigid as she clutched a crucifix

70

in her crossed hands. I shuddered. She was in clown make-up. Was this how a dead body should look? It was too late to wish away my decision to open my eyes. After we had filed by her casket, I discovered that my siblings, like me, had been unable to resist looking at her embalmed body.

Once the funeral Mass began, a priest started swinging brass containers that spilled clouds of incense. That smoke was intense, even a bit sweet, nothing like a campfire. I knew that my father loathed the odor.

My nose wrinkled. *Achoo!* I promptly sneezed.

My father, his brother, and our families sat silently, ramrod straight, throughout the long service. No kneeling, no responses to the priest's liturgy. No receiving Communion. The priest stared sternly at us. The few parishioners in attendance knew the drill: Up, down, up, down. We Elliotts barely budged.

At the end of the Mass, the priest pulled my father and his older brother aside. His face was beet red. "Why didn't your families genuflect? Your mother always talked about what good Catholic boys you were when she raised you." He wiped the moisture from his forehead and above his mouth with the back of his delicate hand. My father drew in his breath.

My Uncle Los shook his head, deferring to Dad. Dad unclasped his hands and said, "Neither of us is Catholic. Neither of us chose to raise our children in the Church." He paused. He looked at his older sibling. Would he elaborate?

He did not. The priest's mouth opened and shut as if he were blowing up a balloon. Without the balloon.

Over most of Dad's life, he rarely reminisced about Grandma Elliott. Nor did we kids, because she'd terrorized us—in life and at her own funeral. Nonetheless, decades later at a family reunion, now in his mid-eighties, Dad was asked about her by his curious great-grandchildren.

"What was she like, Geep?" (Dad's nickname for grandfather was Geep, while Mom's was Geem for grandmother.) Geep shot Geem a look.

He cleared his throat from his brown leather and teak recliner, a Father's Day gift a couple years earlier from Sue, Bud, Joan, and me. Then, he shared a story none of us had heard.

"Was she full of humor? Certainly not. Was she pretty? Not especially. Was she good company? Hardly. But my, she was a force to be reckoned with."

Now, he had everyone's attention. Late in life, my father tapped into Irish storytelling mode. "It was the Depression. My father, a Boston City cop, had rescued someone from drowning. During the rescue, he had himself been injured and had to go on unpaid sick leave. Suddenly, my mother needed to make an income. She submitted a business proposal to the Boston City Parks Commission, bidding to manage the Norumbega Park summer concessions. She signed the requisition as N. H. Elliott, for two reasons. Her first name, Norah, would reveal she was a woman. If that weren't bad enough, her second name, Hurley, was a dead giveaway that she was Irish. Remember, this was the era when ads stated that 'Irish need not apply.'" Glancing around the sunlit room, I wished I had a camera to capture the spellbound expressions. "Well, guess what? She won the bid!"

The great-grandkids and grandkids clapped. "Oooh, a feminist before anyone heard of them," said one.

Dad shook his head. "She was no feminist. She was a wife and mother struggling to make ends meet. But she was clever. Savvy enough to hide both gender and ethnicity. Of course, the decision-makers tried to renege. She wouldn't hear of it. She put Los and me to work on the canoe rentals and ran the music and dance bandstand herself. We worked our asses off and raked in tons of money."

I heard the begrudging admiration in his voice.

Three generations of Elliotts surrounded him in a large circle. The youngest was enthralled. Of course! They'd never met her. When I caught Sue's eye, she grimaced.

Each generation gets to rewrite the family history.

That day, I realized Grandma Elliott had been intelligent. No surprise, since Dad was one of the smartest men I knew. His razor-sharp memory could still recite the middle names of all the vice presidents of the United States, for crying out loud. My little girl eyes had easily discerned that his good looks were inherited from his father. But at fifty-three, I also appreciated what else my crabby grandmother had given him: Grit. Gumption. Resilience.

A NERVOUS BREAKDOWN

EVERYTHING WAS GREAT until it wasn't.

Our family was about to embark on our third trip to visit my mother's parents in Winter Park, Florida.

All six of us, including Brandy, were familiar with the three-day drive. After all, we'd done it when I was five, and again two years later, when I was seven. At those young ages, the long trip had felt like an adventure. We started out on the Atlantic seacoast surrounded by seagulls, trees, and hills and ended up in a flat, sandy, interior expanse of palm trees, alligators, and swamps. How exotic states like South Carolina, Georgia, and Florida sounded coming from my lips, as I traced the state borders in the *World Book Encyclopedia*.

With the passage of a few years, though, school and social activities interested us kids more than a repeat road trip over the same 1,300 miles. Even Mom and Dad were reluctant to pull us out of class for as long as the two weeks in February over Washington and Lincoln's birthday holidays. Fortunately, Grandpa and Grandma Worden had flown north to visit us in the intervening years. Now, though, my grandfather's failing health was keeping them in Florida.

Just before we left, Joan whispered into the space between our twin beds, "Well, Susan for one, is feeling full of herself. She gets to show off her driving skills with her newly minted license."

I banged my pillow with my fist. "Yeah, but only on those godforsaken country roads in the deep South. Still, that gives her more time up front. Which means that Bud, you, and I will sit longer stretches in the back of the car with more turns on the hump."

Joan chuckled. "Yup, my thoughts exactly. I wish we had our driver's licenses, too."

Before drifting off to sleep, I said, "It will be our last time ever, doing this trip as a family. Susan goes off to college this fall. Heck, she's halfway there already in her mind. We'll never be a six-some again. Seven, counting Brandy. It's kind of our last hurrah." The *zzz* sound I heard was my sister, Joan, snoring. Even though she always denied that she snored. Yet again, she'd beaten me to sleep.

That night, Mom and Dad had pulled out the AAA map of the eastern part of the United States, and each put their hand on the place where they'd relinquish the wheel to Susan. "We thought a small detour in Williamsburg would be fun for you kids. There's a lot of history about the South's involvement in the Revolutionary War that we don't hear about in Massachusetts where people focus on Lexington and Concord."

Sue stared, memorizing the spot. "But Williamsburg's so far to the south. Why won't you let me drive sooner than that?"

My father gave her a long look. Hovering near, I thought he looked exhausted. He said, "Well, there's way too much traffic and distractions in the Northeast around the big cities. You'll log easier miles once we reach Williamsburg."

Mom folded up the map before placing it atop the suitcases and sleeping bags lined up by the garage door.

I had fond memories of our two earlier trips. Mom and Dad had pulled us out of several days of school; none of my second-grade classmates had been to Florida. When Miss Cluff gave a class assignment of writing letters to me, I was thrilled. A huge brown package arrived at my grandparents' home, filled with twenty-four handwritten notes. What, they all asked, did I like best about the Sunshine State?

Easy answer! Ha! The oranges! Grandpa Worden had orange trees in his sandy back yard. He'd taken us four kids out back to demonstrate the proper way to extract orange juice. First, he carved a hole in the top of the fruit before taking his pocketknife and carving the peel down to the mid-section. Then, he squeezed the fruit and sucked it into his mouth. "No glass. No mess." We clapped. I was eager to boast about this new skill with friends.

On our first expedition, Mom and Dad arranged a layover in Silver Spring, Maryland with her cousin Roseabelle and her husband, Ian. None of us kids had seen the nation's capital. Ian got into full tour guide mode, driving us around the city during the day and even at night, when famous buildings like the Jefferson Memorial, the Washington Memorial, and the Lincoln Memorial were flood-lighted dramatically. We all skipped up the concrete stairs to gain a close-up look at the somber, sad face of the seated President Lincoln. His expression was weary. I realized that he looked nothing like other famous dead presidents or generals who usually were depicted on horseback or standing tall in uniform. He looked like my father when Kristin Elliott Christmas Cards was in trouble.

On that trip, before we all hit our sleeping bags in Silver Spring, Ian pulled out a cribbage board and a deck of cards. "What? You don't play cribbage? Well, in a few minutes, none of you kids will be able to say that!" Cribbage was an immediate hit and would be a favorite game among all of us Elliott kids.

Later, when on the road again, we'd begged Mom and Dad to stop at a southern chain of eateries called Stuckey's after we passed several billboards declaring, "If it's Stuckey's, it's gotta be good!" After the fourth teaser billboard, my parents relented. "Hey, we can make it quick and turn it into a pit stop," Dad said. As usual, food was not motivation for my father.

Clambering back into the car, Dad pulled out sandwiches from a brown paper bag. He shifted gears and we pulled out of this popular stop. Each of us was chewing on our selection when Mom suddenly shouted, "Eeew!" She dumped her sandwich on the napkin in her lap.

"What is it? Hey, what's the matter?" we yelled.

Dad glanced over and winced. Mom opened her sandwich to reveal a large, black cockroach. At least it didn't seem to be moving. Against the yellow eggs, it dominated the landscape inside the soggy white pieces of bread. Each of us quietly deposited our remaining lunches in the greasy bag that Dad passed around, wiping our mouths. It took a few seconds before we rejiggered the Stuckey's advertising campaign to, "If it's Stuckey's, it's gotta be yucky!"

The Stuckey's incident became family lore. As did the incident in the middle of our last night of driving without a stop on our second trip. Mom and Dad had decided to save money and not pay for two cabins in a AAA-rated, pet friendly motel in South Carolina. By taking turns at the wheel, we'd arrive the following late morning at my grandparents' ranch home. All of us kids had drifted asleep, me in the back seat along with Brandy, Joan, and Bud. *Lick, lick.* I opened my eyes, staring into Brandy's black pupils that were asking for a little love. I glanced beyond her and saw a road sign that said *Brunswick* with an arrow. Then, I patted the dog, readjusted the blanket, and fell back to sleep.

Was it only an hour later that the car came to a full stop at the side of the lonesome road? *Click! Click!* Mom switched on the overhead light, folding the AAA map in her lap. Dad looked stricken as he tapped the wheel. The bright light was a sharp contrast to the pitch black of the scene outside the windows. I heard sighs and groans from my siblings.

"Hey, everyone. We might be a little off the beaten track. Somehow, somewhere, we took the wrong turn," Mom explained. Brandy wagged her tail, hopeful that she was about to go for a walk and sniff around. Bud rolled down his window to peer outside. The air, hot and humid, enveloped the inside of the car, suffocating us. I could see the white line down the median strip of the road until it disappeared. Into what? A swamp? Or woods, perhaps filled with Spanish moss dangling down to the ground? I shivered, imagining its damp crawlers slipping down under my shirt.

Dad said, "Bud, why don't you give Brandy a chance to do her business?" I peered outside. There was no car, no gas station, no anything out there. Nothingness. Dad added, "We'll take a few minutes to figure out what to do. Put the leash on her, in case a raccoon or squirrel grabs her attention."

Bud squeezed out behind Dad, with Brandy hopping happily in tow. Joan, on my other side, was rubbing her eyes. Sue stretched in the front. "Does Brunswick mean anything?" I asked. I quickly added that I'd spotted a sign mentioning it about an hour ago. "It said go to the left."

Mom groaned, "Of course. Here it is." She indicated the spot on the map with her finger. "Somehow, I missed that turn, Charlie."

Dad stopped tapping the wheel. He hit his forehead with a smack. "Honey, I'm the one who missed it! Damn!"

Mom rubbed the back of his neck. She said, "Sweetie, you're tired, driving for such a long spell. It's no one's fault." He turned, offering a grimace.

"Okay, then. Hey, Bud. Time for you both to get back in the car. Good girl, Brandy!" Together, my two-footed brother and our four-footed buddy squeezed in again, forcing us all to move to accommodate them.

"Why are you grinning, Kristin?" Bud asked, as Mom doused the car light.

Mom said, "Well, without your sister's eagle eyes, we might have driven as far as Alabama."

"Or, worse, Mississippi," Dad added. "Thanks to Kristin, we can loop back and only lose a couple hours." I was still smiling in the dark.

Several hours later, we all cheered when we spotted the "Welcome to Florida" sign. The next pause would be a huge orange juice factory. Brandy liked this stop, as she got into dog inspector general mode, sniffing wooden crates and oranges stacked for shipment. The rest of us were eager to start the morning with a free, freshly squeezed glass of orange juice, except Sue, who strained the pulp between her front teeth.

As my nostrils inhaled the sweet citrus odor, I perked up. New aromas of orange blossoms and fragrant Spanish moss! What a contrast to Massachusetts, I thought. The upcoming days underlined how opposite the two states were. We happily debated what to do, starting with taking the car onto the hard sandy beach at Daytona. Driving on the sand was not allowed at West Beach! Having a small highway of cars to cross on the way to pounding waves was exciting. Or we could take a day trip to Cypress Gardens, where Esther Williams, the movie star, was filming *Million Dollar Mermaid*. We ended up watching as she crisscrossed the waterways on water skis, flaunting a fancy Jantzen bathing suit with a matching bathing cap covered with plastic flowers. I couldn't wait until the movie would be released. But our hands-down favorite place? Sulfur Springs, a natural watering hole with the steepest and longest slide-a-shoot ever. Susan, Bud, Joan, and I couldn't get enough of it. We begged to go back. When packing our suitcases at the end of the week, we spotted holes in the fannies of the suits Mom had sewn for us.

These two vacations when I was in grade school had been fun, full of "firsts." Exploring Florida was like being in a foreign land, a flat landscape of sand, sun, and conch shells. It would be another seven years, when in college, that I learned several classmates had taken elaborate family trips to Europe called the Grand Tour. They'd flown on airplanes (I had not) and stayed in luxurious hotels (I had not) and had gone to world-famous sites (I believed much of what Florida offered would rival them). Mom and Dad had made sure that our February family getaways to Florida were fun-packed and sometimes thrilling. We had no inkling that they were done on a strict budget.

But, at thirteen, I wasn't as gleeful at the proposition that we'd make the trek for a third time. What about my friends, my classes, my homework, and sleepovers? The drive down and back took forever. As kids, we'd exhausted the alphabet game and the license plate competition. These games seemed a bit lame now that we were in junior and senior high school.

The eve before our third trip, I wondered about my lack of excitement. Was it only because there would be fewer new things to do and see once there? I realized Mom was worried about her father's health. We knew her father had been advised a few years before to move to Florida for his lungs and his heart. How she missed having them only a few hours away in West Springfield, Massachusetts! Dad also loved Grandpa and Grandma Worden, as they had embraced him into their small family as if he were their second son. Mom felt strongly that we should make this effort because she hadn't seen her parents in a couple of years. Dad had agreed.

While I wasn't as excited for this third, repeated trip to Florida, I was pleased about my parents' plan to detour in Williamsburg, a well-known historic restoration of the capitol under the British rule that had played a key role in the Revolutionary War. It might resemble Massachusetts' Old Sturbridge Village, a historic town where costumed hosts provided demonstrations of rustic farm life in the 1830s.

I briefly wondered where else we'd stop to sleep in the South after our detour to Williamsburg. It was by far the bleakest stretch of driving. In earlier trips, we'd passed desolate farms that grew cotton, where children were walking barefoot in the fields. We'd watched undernourished kids swinging spindly legs over wooden porches, in overalls and rucksack dresses.

"Why aren't they in school?" we chorused.

Mom said, "Their parents are called sharecroppers and they need all-hands-on-deck to work the fields." She sighed.

I persisted, "Why did Stuckey's have separate bathrooms and water fountains that said 'Colored only'?"

Mom bit a nail. "We're in the South. Here, there is out-and-out racial discrimination. Black people are not allowed to pee in the same bathrooms with whites. They can't stay in the same motels. Often, they can't eat in the same restaurants. Or, if they do, they are relegated to a less desirable section."

We all jumped in. "Hey, that's not fair! Why? Why would anyone want to live in the South?"

Mom and Dad glanced at each other. Dad said, "Good question. Your mother and I are against discrimination. While it is less obvious in the North, it still exists. Everywhere in our country, some white people foster feelings that Blacks are inferior. We have a segregated school system back home, in Boston, for example. So, it's not just in the South." Mom nodded her head.

If we stayed at a motel somewhere in Georgia on this upcoming trip, I was pretty sure there would still be no Black people staying in the cabins nearby. Instead, it would be like Washington, DC, where the doorman at the Smithsonian and the woman wiping the cafeteria table were Black. At thirteen, thinking about racial inequality overwhelmed me. I wished I could do something about it.

As we pulled out of our Hale Street narrow driveway, I felt a pang, knowing it would be another two weeks before we'd pull back in. I was looking forward to seeing my grandparents, although aware that this time, they wouldn't be joining us in our activities because of their health concerns. I also felt the pang of missing my friends.

Only a couple of days later, making the turn that led to the center of Williamsburg, I had a bad feeling in the pit of my stomach. Dad was unusually quiet. Mom had spoken to him a couple times without him responding. He muttered, "Be on the lookout for a parking space."

"There's one!" I shouted.

"Just in the nick of time." Dad pulled in and killed the engine. We emptied from the car, leaving the dog behind as she circled the seat and plopped down for a nap. All of us kids skipped up to the ticket kiosk. The imposing House of Burgesses created a panoramic backdrop. Row after row of red brick were flanked by formal gardens with yellow, red, and purple tulips framing it prettily. To my eyes, it was more imposing than New England architecture. It certainly looked grander than Hale Farm. Perhaps only Boston's gold-domed State House could rival it, sitting atop a hill, overlooking the city. I glanced around, wondering what was taking Mom and Dad so long.

I stared, watching Dad cling onto Mom. Not in a romantic way. She was guiding him to a wooden bench. Then, she walked briskly toward us.

"Susan, here's some money. We won't be taking this tour with you. Your father needs to catch his breath. Go with your brother and sisters. At the end, look for us back here."

Susan pocketed the bill in her jacket, falling into her natural role as first born, the adult with three lesser mortals. (When designated our babysitter, she'd relished threatening us with Dad's hairbrush.) Bud kept his distance from all his sisters, standing a few feet away. He seemed fully aware that he was the only boy amidst three girls. Well, not girls exactly. Sisters!

I leaned over to Joan. "Why does Dad need to rest?"

She tugged on my sleeve. "Mom will figure it out. Everything's gonna be okay. Let's follow her orders." My insides felt queasy. My stomach was roiling.

Even so, when the prettily costumed guide began her spiel, I became enthralled. These were picture-perfect 1770s southern landholder surroundings. Here, wealthy Virginia legislators governed before declaring themselves independent from Britain. They dressed in velvet and lace to twirl on the dance floor at lavish cotillions. In a white cotton cap, with a long, flowered muslin dress, this young guide mischievously pointed out the Necessary, beyond the building. "Isn't our forefathers' term clever for a bathroom?" she asked. I decided their name was more to the point than our term, "restroom."

The guide held one arm up toward the chandeliers that held hundreds of burning candles that cast a flattering light over the silk wallpaper, brocaded curtains, and velvet couches. However, she said nothing about the slaves who worked behind the scenes in this impressive chamber. Instead, the guide highlighted the state's colorful statesman, Patrick Henry, as he incited his countrymen against the British. His clarion call of "Give me liberty or give me death" changed the course of Virginia history, she concluded.

With his words in mind, I went outside into bright sunlight. Immediately, my thoughts turned to Dad. Would he be better? What was wrong with him, exactly?

He was still sitting in the same spot on the bench. Mom was rubbing his back. Then, he put his face in his hands, as if he might throw up.

Hearing our shoes crunch on the gravel walk, Mom looked up at our four worried faces. "Your father isn't any better."

When I glanced at him, Dad's face looked moist, his Celtic skin pasty. "I'm taking him to a doctor. You children grab lunch in the restaurant across the street. Here's more money, Sue. We'll catch up with you here."

We stood by helplessly as Mom walked him slowly to the car, helping him maneuver into the passenger side. Brandy was hopping from back to front, thrilled to be reunited with loved ones.

Susan looked pale. She looked down at the large bills that Mom had pressed into her hand before putting them into a pocket. She brushed her sweaty forehead with the back of her hand. Then, she rallied. "C'mon, you three. Let's skidoo. We have our marching orders. And, we have some real money."

There were plenty of tables now that the two p.m. tours were beginning. We plunked down at a wooden trestle table with deacon's chairs, that reminded us of home. Susan was biting the inside of her lip. Bud was avoiding eye contact. Joan squeezed my hand under the table. I slipped into my customary worrywart manner.

"Order up," Susan said. We shrugged and went for the fried chicken. And, then we all said yes when the waitress, dressed in her Williamsburg garb, suggested sides of French fries.

Popping a French fry into catsup, I asked, "Do any of you know what's going on?"

Bud shrugged. "Well, you don't have to be a genius to see that Dad feels like shit. And he looks like it, too."

Joan's cheek twitched. She was close to tears. "That's obvious. But why, all of a sudden? It's not like he caught a bug. We're all healthy."

Sue agreed. "I'm sure Dad will rebound after seeing the doctor. We have to be patient until they return."

I pressed my back into the chair rail until it hurt. At least it let me think about something other than my father's meltdown. I decided to consider William and Mary as a possible college to apply to. All the buildings resembled a movie set, in which, of course, I pictured myself the star, clothed in a long, silk gown, traipsing among the red tulips and yellow daffodils. Holding my dress up so it wouldn't get stained with the dirt, before bumping into . . . Patrick Henry. He'd be nonplussed. Nonetheless, he'd be captivated by my dainty waistline and my blue eyes.

My daydream ended abruptly. Mom was making her way to our table. Her face was flushed, her eyes red-rimmed. She had not refreshed her lipstick, an ominous sign. Where was Dad?

The waitress in her colonial uniform reappeared, asking Mom if she wanted anything. She looked like she was going to put her hand on Mom's shoulder. Instead, she said, "Honey, I highly recommend today's soup special. It's good for what ails you. Split pea, the chef's special."

"Black coffee only, please." Mom looked up at the waitress. "Well, okay. That soup's my favorite. Give me a bowl of split pea." Mom ran dry fingers through her tousled hair. Then, she itched the back of her hand. It was red, inflamed.

"Where's Dad?" Bud demanded. The rest of us sat still, holding our breath.

"Don't worry, honey. The nice doctor helped me usher Dad into his front office after he'd stumbled going up the steps. It seems that your father's weight has dropped to 119, too low for a man almost six feet tall. The doctor told him to regain twenty pounds in the next few weeks. For now, Dad needs rest. That means staying here."

86

I looked down into my lap. Stick around for how long before heading south to Grandma and Grandpa Worden's? Or stick around here for the rest of our Washington and Lincoln's vacation weeks?

As it turned out, in two days, we'd do a U-turn and head back north. For now, Mom was sipping her soup, as if mind-reading our faces. She filled us in on the abrupt change of plans. "I've already talked to my parents. They'll miss us terribly this winter, but they understand. Your father needs to be home in his own bed. Watch, I'll tempt him with home-cooked meals. He'll be up 'n at 'em before we know it." Her nail-bitten fingers brushed across her dry lips.

Home? I wondered. My dad lying around in bed? I sat, stunned, hands tucked underneath my fanny. Somehow, in the last few hours, my world had shifted. I sensed that whatever was wrong with my always thin father would not be cured by macaroni and cheese or meatloaf. I'd also done the mental calculation comparing Dad's weight to my own. How could he weigh a mere twenty-three pounds more than I did? My father was sick, but not in a way that the doctor here could make him well. My always reliable father had fallen apart. Like Humpty Dumpty. Would he ever get all the broken pieces back together?

Bud's mouth opened. After glancing at Mom's distraught face, he squelched his question. Maybe, he too, was adding up the new configuration of our family. Without Dad in the lead role, Bud would have to play "man of the house." Sue hugged Mom. Joan was fuzzing her arm when I glanced her way.

Mom put the spoon down, not finishing the soup. She slipped a bill under her plate and wiped her mouth with the cloth napkin. "Dad and Brandy are already checked into the motel nearby, waiting for us. Tomorrow, you'll do more sightseeing.

We'll all take off after breakfast the following day. By then, Dad will be more himself. Susan, what a godsend that you'll share the driving." Susan managed a smile, but my mother did not.

I couldn't stop thinking about Dad. He'd always been thin. But now, he was way too skinny. How had none of us noticed? I'd considered my father a gentleman, one who quietly took charge. He protected us as a family and loved us all. He also managed our family business in partnership with Mom. Somehow, he had not taken charge of his own health. Somehow, even Mom had been taken unawares.

We kids filled our sightseeing day with a variety of Williamsburg offerings—tours of impressive buildings and cooking demonstrations. It was like going to the movies and falling asleep. I remember few specifics of how we passed our time. Quickly, I shed my daydream of a starring role with Patrick Henry in the opposite lead. No, I'd never return here to go to William and Mary College. Why would I? It would be a silent testimony, reminding me of this family crisis, the horrible day when Dad had stopped, half dead, in his tracks.

After we checked out of the motel, I saw that Dad wasn't sitting behind the wheel of the car as was his habit whenever we began a road trip. Instead, he'd positioned himself in the front passenger seat, extending it as far back as possible. Like a patient in bed, I thought, as Mom tucked a blanket around his thin torso. The shortest-legged person sat behind him— me. What scared me most was how feeble he looked, lying still. My world turned upside down. I was pretty sure that Dad wouldn't die, but he was the palest I'd seen him.

I had a flashback to my fright when looking at Grandma Elliott in her coffin. When Mom put the station wagon in reverse without easing the clutch smoothly the way Dad always did, I felt a shift in my psyche. Would Dad ever be Dad again?

Decades later, I have scarce memory of the return home from this aborted vacation. Somehow, the heroic tag team of Mom and Susan got us back through the major highways around Washington, DC, Baltimore, Philadelphia, New York City, and Hartford. Finally, to home.

What do I remember? I felt shocked, watching Dad stumble upstairs, holding onto the railing like an old man. He left us to unpack the contents of the car. For days, he did not leave the master bedroom. We spoke in whispers, as if living under the roof with a dying man. Mom made multiple trips up and down the stairs, with offerings of snacks, returning with plates barely touched. Her expression was grim. She drove Dad to appointments, mostly to the doctor. We heard murmurings of the term "nervous breakdown."

At night, she'd flop down on her back on the hooked rug in the den, next to her office desk. Her skin had developed itchy red patches around her scalp and her hands, a condition called eczema. She also started getting headaches, making her face pinch up. "Kristin, please give me one of your wonderful head massages. Your strong fingers soothe my forehead." Her smile was upside down as I sat on the floor above her head, cross-legged. I could help soothe the pain inside her head but not the ache in her heart.

Mom had been doing double duty as much as she could, filling in for Dad's absence. She had always worked at home, doing the clerical work and art buying, as well as taking care of us kids. Now, she was trying to fill in on Dad's end, but she couldn't divide herself in two, with one self going to The Other Place (our nickname for Dad's plant on the other side of town) to pack and ship orders neatly boxed by Janet, Grace, and Gerry, and another self, based at home. Early one morning, I lingered on the landing outside our upstairs bathroom, near their bedroom. I noticed the door wasn't fully shut. They were talking in low tones. Of course, I eavesdropped.

Mom said, "You can't lie here day after day, Charlie. You have to get up and go back to work. They need you at The Other Place. Hell, we need you here. I'm proud that you have the guts to see a shrink. But those sessions won't produce an overnight cure. Meanwhile, there's work to do. So, here are my terms."

I shifted from one foot to the other, aware the wooden landing outside their door might squeak. Should I tiptoe away? My dread for what was to come kept me in place, holding my breath.

Mom continued, "If you refuse to get dressed, to even do a few simple tasks like picking up the mail at the P.O., or to show up at The Other Place, I will pack up and leave you. I'll take the kids and the dog with me. So, it's up to you."

I put my fist inside my mouth to muffle an outburst. I couldn't let them know that I'd been listening. Then I bit down hard to make my pain distract me from Mom's threat. What she had suggested felt like a punch in my gut. I could never picture her dragging us with her while leaving Dad to fend for himself. I felt sorry for him. He was so helpless. Even so, I wanted to pound my fists on his chest and shout at him, echoing my mother. What would he say to her?

"Betsy, give me a little more time. Don't ever say that you'll leave me. Not now. Never, ever. I'd just as soon die." There was a long silence. Then, I heard soft sobs. Was it Mom? Dad? It might have been both.

Whether a ploy or for real, Mom's ultimatum worked results. Within days, like Lazarus, Dad rose from his sickbed,

90

dressed himself in his chino pants, now with a leather belt to cinch them closer around his scrawny waist. He chose a starched white cotton Oxford shirt for his debut at breakfast. All of us averted our eyes as he chewed slowly, ever so slowly, on one piece of toast with peanut butter. I could eat that in three seconds! For him, it required five minutes.

He also continued to faithfully keep weekly appointments with a psychiatrist, along with checkups with the family doctor. Our parents explained that Dad's breakdown wasn't just about being run down. He suffered from depression and needed to learn how to deal with it. The sessions were private, so Dad didn't go into detail. Mom did say that many people with mental illness were ashamed. In fact, she added, men would often avoid seeing a psychiatrist, considering it a sign of weakness. Mom said, "We should be proud of your father for taking this brave step."

Gradually, Dad's belt expanded a notch. His Celtic complexion regained its ruddiness. Once again, I heard him laugh.

It didn't take an Einstein to realize that Dad got up every day thinking the glass was half empty. Mom, by contrast, believed the glass was half full. Did some of this mental health crisis have to do with guilt and our Grandma Elliott? I knew enough to realize that just because a person dies doesn't mean her spirit might not haunt you. Did any of Dad's depression have to do with his flunking out of Harvard Medical School and not becoming a doctor?

Like my siblings, I could only guess. To this day, when I reflect on Dad's nervous breakdown—the diagnostic term used in the 1950s and 1960s—I marvel at his recovery. He'd made a bold move by breaking from the stereotype that strong men don't lie down in a therapist's office to spill their guts.

Even so, I doubted that he'd defeated all his demons. During junior high and high school and well into college, I'd peer at him out of the corner of my eye. I worried when he pushed the French fries around his plate. I worried when he said he was bushed but no one else was. I worried during Wellesley College's Sophomore Father's Weekend, afraid he might not make it through all three sets of tennis. I held my breath as he almost staggered to the net to shake hands with our competition. Not letting me down had taken a physical toll on him.

As I matured, I decided that Dad had found a halfway place to keep anxiety at bay though I was never again privy to my parents' pillow talk. At the time, I'd shared what I'd overheard with my siblings. Each digested it differently, depending on gender and order of rank. I'm not sure if any of them were as disturbed as I was. After all, I'd been the eavesdropper. I'd been the one to hear the distress when Dad begged Mom to never leave him.

Somehow, for the rest of his life, Dad suppressed his anxiety enough to keep going. He got up early, ate breakfast with us, and drove to the P.O. and on to The Other Place. He pitched in with my mother to build a brick patio behind the kitchen. He taught my siblings how to drive. He attended Bud's JV basketball games some evenings. Once in a while, he hit the tennis ball in the public court behind our house with Joan and me. He went every year to Mt. Holyoke College for their annual Fathers' Weekend. The family business grew.

For me, part of his legacy was an ability to move on, despite the demons. While doing so, he held close those whom he held dear: My mother, Susan, Bud, Joan, and me. Even Brandy.

Would Mom ever have walked away from him, taking us in tow? Who was she kidding? She'd sooner have left us than Dad.

Theirs was a love match. They were partners in every sense, in business as well as in marriage. Of course, being Mom, she took some credit for Dad's recovery. I was forever grateful that she was such a convincing actress.

NO WORDS

THE MAGIC OF WORDS permeated our household. Mom and Dad were avid readers of *The Boston Globe* and the *Beverly Evening Times*. Despite the demands of the business, they found time to read John Cheever, F. Scott Fitzgerald, and Truman Capote. On Mom's bedside table sat Ernest Hemingway's *The Old Man and the Sea*, counterbalanced by Robert Traver's *Anatomy of a Murder* on Dad's side. Sometimes, Mom would joke that her best uninterrupted reading came when sitting on the john with the door closed.

I still remember my excitement when, in grade school, my parents announced that they'd saved enough money to purchase *The World Book Encyclopedia*. When the huge set arrived, Mom carefully unpacked the heavy cartons to display the handsome royal-blue hardcover volumes, each embossed in white letters from A to Z. I loved picking up a volume to read out loud about random topics to our terrier, Brandy, or to myself. After the set arrived, we made fewer walks up the blocks to the marble steps of the Beverly Public Library to research questions that our curious minds posed at all times of the day and night.

Happily, my reading habit began at an early age. My two childhood prized possessions were a library card and a Beverly Savings Bank book. (Dad always drove Joan and me downtown and accompanied us to the teller's booth. There, the bank employee stamped our books to add our deposit to our growing balance of hard-earned dollars. Walking outside, we two felt like grown-ups.)

Around age six, I didn't need an adult to escort me to the library. It was fun to walk or bike up the short distance from our house with my sister Joan or a friend to borrow books, books, and more books. As many as my bike basket would carry. Of course, as the youngest, I wanted to read what my older siblings were reading. Mom and Dad also subscribed to a variety of popular magazines, including *Time*, *The Saturday Evening Post*, *The Saturday Review*, *The New Yorker*, and *McCall's*. The 1950s were the golden era of these publications. Well-established writers like John Updike and John O'Hara published stories in their pages, which we consumed, cover to cover, along with the non-fiction and novels that my parents read. One time, an eighth-grade teacher overheard me talking with a friend about *Butterfield 8* and pulled me aside. "That author, John O'Hara, writes racy stuff. Does your mother know you're reading him?"

I looked up at her pursed lips. "Well, actually, Mom loaned me the book and told me to read it quickly, before the library expiration date," I said. Miss Trout looked surprised as she released her hand from my shoulder. I turned my head so she wouldn't see my smirk as I caught up to friends hurrying to our next class.

Mom had a strong desire to get published in a national magazine. How she finagled time out from the business to write romance short stories, I will never know. Long after my bedtime, her fingers danced over the typewriter keys, as she converted her neat writing—the same script she'd used for the name of the card company—from lined paper pads into rows of type. Thick manilla envelopes filled with her pristine manuscripts and cover letters got tucked under Dad's arm when he was en route to the P.O.

One day, sitting in the den watching TV, I'd heard the *thwap, thwap* of the metal letter box in the front door. It was opening and shutting to allow the mail through the slot. *Whoosh, whoosh!* Magazines spilled over the hall floor. *Whoosh,* envelopes tumbled in. Last, a return envelope, in her handwriting, which she'd thoughtfully included with her submission. Mom spotted it right away and jumped from her chair to retrieve it. After she opened it, she sat down. And sighed.

"Mom, what did the editor say?" I asked.

"It's a no. But this editor is encouraging me to send it back, after a revision. Which is probably still a rejection, but at least it's a kind one," she said.

How I wished her hope would come to fruition. But it never did. Nonetheless, Mom's persistence was remarkable. She'd chew on her bottom lip and sharpen her pencil, absorbed in the romance between her two lead characters. Once in a while, she'd read a small section out loud to me, but not often. She might ask if the writing sounded good. I didn't know how it compared to O'Hara or Updike, but it sounded pretty good to me. "Of course!" I'd say.

Her best friend, Ruth, pointed out that if she had wanted the dream enough to make it a reality, she would have carved out more time. But I never saw it that way. My mother was busy taking care of our family and the business. When, exactly, I would have challenged Ruth, was Mom going to find even more precious hours? Just because she didn't have more time to write didn't mean that she didn't want her ambition to be realized.

Decades later, Mom put aside her manuscripts and picked up paintbrushes and an easel. I found her new passion wonderful. Throughout her business career, she'd always enjoyed collaborating with artists. More than once, she'd put on her artist beret after purchasing a design that she thought needed a kick-in-the-pants. She'd squint an eye and mutter that the design should be more eye catching. Then, she'd carefully apply a red pen to fill in a Santa's cap. Or draw a stocking to hang over a mantel. Becoming an artist in her seventies seemed like a natural progression. Her subjects reflected her love of nature and animals: yellow tulips; red roses; orange pumpkins; her calico cat, Patches; Rice's Beach and beyond; sailboats heading back into Beverly Harbor.

If the hubbub at 57 Dane Street, and later, at 176 Hale Street, might have been distracting for an aspiring fiction writer, it was clearly the favorite hangout for all our friends. In 1950, Mom and Dad decided to splurge and buy a black and white television. Who didn't want to come over on Saturdays to watch *The Cisco Kid* and *The Lone Ranger*? A few years later, our circa 1770s house in the Cove boasted a basketball hoop over the barn door, a badminton net behind it, and croquet wickets in the yard outside the kitchen. Indoors, hooked rugs welcomed bodies stretched over the floor to play Monopoly or Clue. My eighth-grade friends were amazed when they watched my mother type. They appreciated her crackerjack skill, having endured our classroom drill of closing our eyes while typing *the quick brown fox jumped over the lazy dog,* the iconic exercise that includes every letter of the alphabet. She epitomized the quick brown fox! Not surprisingly, my childhood and adolescent memories are mingled with the sound of typewriter keys being struck, the carriage being returned with a bang, and the paper being whipped out of the machine.

Friends lucky enough to wrangle a supper invitation to our house were flattered if Mom or Dad asked them questions to "pick their brains" for ideas. Should they expand the card line beyond Christmas themes? Maybe consider gift wrapping paper? Everyday greeting cards? Cookbooks? Meals got boisterous as meatloaf was passed, and friends pitched ideas into the air like badminton shuttlecocks. In the advertising world, these suggestions might be called brainstorming. In our home, they were a normal part of dinner table conversation.

The chatter at home spilled over to the plant at 50 Rear Rantoul, where two friends of my parents became long-time employees. Grace and Janet boxed cards the way my mother typed orders—accurately, and with high energy. No one could count to twenty-five faster than Grace, even if she was reciting the menu from dinner last night. No one could put plastic lids on boxes more quickly than Janet, even while sharing the trick her basset hound, Crumpet, just learned. Their arthritic hands, speckled with brown age spots, flew over cards like croupiers dealing chips in a Las Vegas casino. Here, at the Kristin Elliott plant, their agile fingers counted cards, envelopes, boxes, and ditty bags for shipment to retailers. Their highest praise for us, the children of the owner? "Charlie, your girls count in twenty-fives almost as fast as we do."

How much quieter was it in the back shipping room. There, Dad and Bud worked side by side, with a radio broadcasting Boston's WBZ news station softly in the background. Theirs was a camaraderie that required little chit-chat. Was it partly because Dad was never one to be talkative? Or was it because of a male female division of labor when it came to conversation?

Over dinner one night, when each of us was recounting our school day, my brother slapped the wooden table. "Hey, give a guy a break! I'm trying to get a word in edgewise. Impossible when all you women talk at once. How about letting me finish a sentence? There's only two of us to the four of you."

My father raised an eyebrow. His lips curved into a slight smile. "Bud, you may need to learn how to express yourself better than by pounding the table. We'd be delighted to hear what's on your mind. Most times, I'm content to sit back and listen to the back-and-forth."

Perhaps because she was taking off next year for college, Susan entered the fray. "That sounds like you issued us a direct challenge, Bud. We're up for it, aren't we?" She looked around the table to Mom, Joan, and me. We were nodding our heads. "How about we four not speak any words this coming Saturday? We can use gestures and make up sounds. But . . . no words! Of course, you and Dad can talk to your heart's content. Got it?"

Bud cocked his head, looking for the catch. It sounded like a slam dunk. No interruptions. Bliss! He glanced at Dad. Again, that glimmer of a smile.

"Okay, sure," said Bud. "Winners of the men against the women challenge pick their favorite lunch menu. I can already taste all the BLT's that I'll snarf down. Yum!" Bud was smacking his lips. Dad, on the other hand, never had an appetite for a meal and often left small portions uneaten. He'd never be motivated by the lure of food. Was he winking at Mom?

We women snickered as we cleared the table, rinsing dishes for the dishwasher. Bud looped a garbage bag over his shoulder to take out to the barn. Dad stepped outside, to probably sneak a Pall Mall. No matter how many times he had cut back, he'd never totally quit the habit. Possibly, I thought, he and Bud would discuss a Saturday game strategy. Mostly, I was happy that he agreed to our challenge. His breakdown had taken a toll on his sense of humor.

"Who cares who gets the BLT lunch?" said Sue. "I just want to outsmart them. That's the real point."

Saturday morning, I awaited my turn in the upstairs bathroom. Susan popped out, holding the creaky wooden door open. She put her finger to her lips. I didn't need her nonverbal signal. I'd been lying awake in bed imagining breakfast. How would it go? I was sure we girls could count on each other and Mom not to trip up. Unless Bud had a trick up his sleeve. One meal at a time, I told myself.

I ran the faucet to brush my teeth. *Gurgle, guzzle.* Stepping from the bathroom out into the hall, behind Mom and Dad's bedroom door, I overheard Dad saying, "I'm headed downstairs to let Brandy out."

Usually, Mom would respond, reminding him to start the coffee. This morning, all she replied was, "Mmmm."

I could hear the click as Dad unlocked the heavy downstairs back door. He said in his man-to-dog voice, "There you go. Such a good girl."

Descending the stairs, I expected to see Dad measuring the Maxwell House ground coffee into the glass percolator. Instead, he'd followed Brandy out to the barn. The siren song of smoking. Did he really believe that none of us knew he had not kicked this addiction? He'd vacated the non-talking kitchen staging area, so Bud had to soldier it alone.

"Hey, was that the sound of elephant feet that beat me down the stairs, Kristin?" Bud's provocative insult was meant to get a rise out of me. I stared back, rewarded by his sticking out his tongue. *So mature, Bud*, I wanted to taunt him. I zipped my lips. On the carpeted steps behind him, Susan, Joan, and Mom followed. Each greeted him with a *harrum* and *harramph*, guttural good-morning salutations. His eyes darted out the kitchen window to the driveway, where Dad rubbed out a cigarette with the sole of his shoe. "Good morning to you. Prepare to lose," he said. His finger tapped nervously on his empty milk glass. Somehow, he did not appear as brazen as his words.

When Dad came back in and joined us at the table, Mom handed him the Sports section of the *Globe*. That got his attention as did her radiant smile. "You're looking like the cat that swallowed the canary, Betsy. Now, tell me, why is that?"

She shrugged and moved toward the stove to make coffee. How pretty she looked even without her first cup of coffee or an application of lipstick. Her eyes shone with the day's challenge. Meanwhile, all of us sisters kept busy pulling down Cheerios, Wheat Chex, or retrieving the Hood's milk bottle and the pitcher of Minute Maid orange juice prepared the night before. Mom was now humming, "I'm Gonna Wash That Man Right Outa My Hair" from *South Pacific*, keeping the beat to the percolating coffee.

Abruptly, Mom whacked the front page of the paper. "*Karoomph! Kerumm!*" Another noise akin to a cough sputtered deep within her throat. We looked up over our cereal bowls as she held up the headline, announcing that there was a growing crisis over the status of West Berlin in the Cold War.

Dad said, "Oh, shit. An escalation with a war of words. Only this is for real, unlike the small-scale war going on inside our house."

Joan, Susan, and I kept our lips sealed. We invented distressed noises resembling a vacuum cleaner on high hitting a bobby pin. *Varoosh!* Russia's ultimatum to the Western Powers to withdraw from Berlin might have backfired if Khrushchev had tapped the non-military might of the Elliott women.

In the long pause following our grunts and groans, I got up to refill the coffee. Both parents drank their coffee black. No need for any words.

This first test of the day was a breeze. What if a neighbor or a stranger had popped in? Would they think the women had lost the ability to speak? Or that we'd lost our minds, what with our hands gesturing, fists punching into the newspaper, fingers pointing up, down, and sideways, with an accompaniment of grunting?

Mercifully, no one needed a cup of sugar that day.

We kids scattered. Bud appeared with a basketball and announced, "Off to Tony's to shoot hoops. Home for lunch." But Bud still hung around, hoping we'd be tempted to blurt out a word or two.

Sue waved good-bye, but not before uttering, "*Urghh!*" Then, she gestured down the street to Liz's house and made her fingers march like sticks. Mom gave her the thumbs up.

Brring, brring! Contest rules did not apply outside our family unit. Over the phone, I told Terry not to come here; I'd head over to her house. Overhearing me, Mom nodded with another thumbs up. Joan's turn, under Bud's watchful eye. "*Umph!*" She zig-zagged her fingers over the trestle table to its opposite side and then a sharp left, mimicking the direction of the weed-filled path behind our barn that ended near her friend Ann's house. Mom laughed. "*Humum. Deedum.*"

Dad watched, transfixed. "Guess I won't ask if anyone wants to run down to the P.O. with me this morning, since everyone has plans. And no way we could converse." He added, "Well, I could talk to myself. I certainly don't comprehend the grunting. Or the hand gestures. It's as if you have a secret language." He chuckled as he exited with his car keys. A moment later, he popped back. "Betsy, I'll head over to The Other Place this morning. Get a few orders packed. Back by noon for another installment of No Words."

Close to noon, I told Terry I needed to leave early to confab with my sisters and mother. She asked, "How long will you go on grunting, pointing, and squeaking?"

"As long as it takes. Bud and Dad seem perplexed, Bud more than Dad. He couldn't wait to vamoose following breakfast, after making sure none of us cheated. But this challenge was all his doing!"

Terry laughed. I suspected she harbored a secret crush on my brother.

I ran the four blocks home, eager to continue the contest. Mom was bent over the broiler, toasting Pepperidge Farm white bread for BLTs. Was she letting the men know that everyone wanted the same outcome from the challenge? I grabbed a knife to begin slicing ripe tomatoes.

Mom said, "While there are no men present, my gut says that lunch may be the end of the gender challenge. Your father is amused by the goings on. Bud, on the other hand? He seems dazed."

We made an assembly line of crisp bacon strips, washed lettuce, and sliced tomatoes. At the tail end, a mayonnaise jar with a knife plopped into it sat adjacent to stacks of toast. Salt and pepper shakers on the table. Joan grabbed six lunch plates. Sue poured milk.

In my eyes, my father was the silent type. Up until his nervous breakdown, I'd compared him favorably to John Wayne, whom I adored in the classic movie *The Quiet Man*. "Actions speak louder than words," might have been his credo. Mostly, Dad watched. The little that he said was notable.

"Since Bud and Dad are due to arrive any minute, I want to make a quick observation," Sue said. "At breakfast, Bud looked like a lost puppy." She sounded gleeful, as if primed for victory. Joan and I exchanged glances. We four were a competitive bunch, I realized, so close in age. Not one of us liked to lose.

We heard Dad pull the Plymouth station wagon into the driveway. The engine cut out. Then, he shouted, "Hey, Bud! Good timing. Let's go in and mount a solid front against the loyal opposition." He wrapped his arm around Bud's shoulder, which was unusual. He was not demonstrative and less so since the Williamsburg debacle.

Bud announced, "I'm starving . . . worked up an appetite playing ball. My shooting is in top form. Maybe it's a sign we'll have a good JV season. And a sign that victory is now at hand."

"Hope you're right on both counts, Bud," said Dad. The two of them shouted out hellos and howdies to us.

Bud said, "Wow! My favorite! And we haven't earned them yet!"

Dad said, "My favorite, too, Betsy. I'll have my usual one and be done."

Bud clapped his hands, "All the more for me!" Mom handed him a plate, waving him toward the ingredients, lined up for self-assembly.

Bud was eager to consume as many BLTs as a sixteen-year-old hoopster could, guaranteeing lunch would be more than a fifteen-minute sit down. All the while, we gals harumphed and gesticulated. I clinked my glass and raised it, in a toast to Mom for her lunch treat. Throughout, we women giggled at our extravagant hand gestures and guttural commentary. Many times, to tease them, we pointed at Dad and Bud, indicating it was their turn to speak.

Bud asked Dad if he'd picked up much business when he went to the P.O. Box this morning. Dad shook his head. "Not much, but spring isn't the busiest time of year." Bud stared at Sue who didn't blink. Next Joan. Finally, me. Usually, we'd chime in, asking Dad to elaborate. Was Bud daring us? We did not rise to the bait.

By his fourth sandwich, Bud was slowing down. He threw down his napkin. Standing up, he said, "Game over. Not even close to a tie. You women win. I can't stand the grunts and groans, wheezes. They're worse than words. It's like living in the novel *Animal Farm*. Somehow, you manage to communicate with each other. I prefer your talking over each other to this snorting festival."

We sisters broke into spontaneous applause, giggling with each other and Mom.

Dad said, "Bud, we never stood a chance. Someday, you may realize that women have a secret language beyond words. It involves non-verbal gestures. It may be intuitive. Or learned behavior. But men? We struggle simply to keep up."

Bud plunked down again to finish his last sandwich, mulling over Dad's commentary. I was sure he loved BLT's too much to forever associate them with our No Words challenge.

As for me, *bacon, lettuce, and tomato* always conjures up our female victory in our family war of No Words, along with the promise of my favorite sandwich.

The initials BLT say it all—no words needed!

THE HUSBAND TEST

SATURDAY MORNINGS, Dad performed the ritual of going to the post office to empty the contents of PO Box 23, owned by Kristin Elliott Cards. He and Mom kept close tabs on sales generated by company reps across the country.

Had I been blindfolded, I think that I could have walked from the massive front door of the P.O. and across the vast chamber to Box 23. For Mom and Dad, its contents were more valuable than the Crown Jewels. The folders and envelopes inside contained orders and checks from department stores, bookshops, boutiques, and sales reps. A box chockablock full was their definition of treasure.

Sometimes, Dad might head further down Rantoul Street from the P.O. to gas up at the Mobil station owned by Nick. If there was a pressing order to ship, he'd make the four-block detour to finalize the shipment, getting it off his to-do list. At

The Other Place, everyone adhered to the mantra: *If you have a job to do, do it now.*

By the time we kids came down into the kitchen, Dad usually had the coffee percolating and the Pepperidge Farm English Muffins in the toaster. Cereal boxes were out on the counter next to the Hood's milk and Minute Maid orange juice for helping ourselves. Dad usually had only one half of a muffin unless Mom prodded him to eat more.

I'd watch them divide *The Boston Globe*, with Dad getting his favorite section, Sports. Over his first cup of black coffee, he'd say, "Well, the good news is that I don't know anyone in the Obits today." He often referred to the Obituaries as the "Irish Sports Pages."

"Why?" I asked, baffled. What was so engrossing about people dying?

He chuckled. "Once you reach a certain age, you dread seeing a write-up about a friend or acquaintance." Dad was only forty-five. Even at thirteen, I knew the Irish were stereotyped as maudlin. Dad was only half-Irish but at moments like this, he seemed 100 percent Irish.

Then, having survived the potential tragedy of the obits, Dad would turn to the real sports section, with a sigh of relief. This part of the paper he enjoyed, often with a smile. The blow-by-blow description of the previous day's Boston Red Sox double header against the despised New York Yankees merited a fist bump with Bud. A win for the Sox, accompanied by multiple hits from his favorite team member, #9, Ted Williams, was a win for my father.

Lately, Dad had started to track the career of Arnold Palmer, an athlete who played another of his favorite sports, golf. Our family lore included the footnote that Dad's golf game had been good enough for him to consider turning pro himself. As a teenager, he'd earned good money caddying at a prestigious golf course near his hometown, Waltham. He'd sharpened his game enough to consider earning a living playing the circuit. When we kids pestered him why he hadn't, he laid out his three reasons.

First, he said, there was the Depression. Even in good times, it was a long shot to become a pro. He compared it to heading for Hollywood to become a movie star. "And I'm no Cary Grant," he said. It was steady, reliable work that men were supposed to seek in the 1930s.

Second, he elaborated, he was from a poor family, with a father who was a Boston City cop and a mother who'd crossed the Atlantic from County Roscommon, Ireland. The Professional Golf Association didn't welcome players of immigrant family stock. It was the *Irish Need Not Apply* rule yet again.

Third, (and I realized that my father often framed issues in terms of threes), country clubs were exclusive, welcoming only white men, usually of privilege. "That's not the world I live in," he said.

He shrugged it off. "Who knows? I probably wouldn't have made the cut." Which convinced me that he would have.

After breakfast, we kids would begin to peel away, finding friends to play with. Dad would always go into the den to have a word with Mom at her typewriter before leaving. Her fingers were flying at ninety words a minute, and she barely paused as he leaned over her shoulder to ask, "Any grocery item you need me to pick up at Givonni's coming home?"

She'd smile, nodding her head no, lining up the sales numbers in a column, juggling several carbon copies. "No thanks,

Charlie. I'm all set. See you in a bit." He might squeeze her shoulder before heading out to the car.

I remember one particular Saturday I had my usually reserved father all to myself. I heard the repetitive *bang, bang* of Bud's practice shots against the basketball hoop on the barn door. Then, he took off for a pick-up game at a friend's house. Joan had left on a walk with two Beverly Cove friends. Susan wasn't part of our Saturdays or any other days anymore, now away in South Hadley, Massachusetts, as a freshman at Mt. Holyoke College.

When Dad asked if anyone wanted to accompany him, I yelled, "Yes!"

Predictably, Mom was multi-tasking in the den, humming while typing and glancing at the news on the television. When Dad asked if she needed him to run an errand, she shook her head no. "Off you go. You two have fun."

How in the world, I wondered, could she look over her shoulder, smile, and not make an error?

Brushing a few crumbs of toast from my T-shirt, I sat down on the passenger side of the station wagon. Dad had already opened the door for me and then shut it before settling in behind the wheel.

This morning, he'd also toot down to Nick's gas station to fill up his almost empty tank. Okay by me, I thought. Oddly, I enjoyed inhaling the smell of gasoline. Who knew then that benzene was noxious and cancer producing? Looking back, I'm guessing that the sweet, pungent odor provided a childhood high. Besides that small pleasure, I also liked Nick, the ruddy-faced service station owner who greeted each Elliott by name. He usually winked at me when nobody was looking. Except me.

I watched Dad easily maneuver the tight space between our 1770s colonial and its adjacent 1740s parent. Hopefully, we joked, the two original families got along well, living in such close proximity. When we lived there, Susan could lean out her second-story bedroom window and throw spitballs to the neighbor in the bedroom opposite hers. Neither had to be that good a shot to land a direct hit.

This morning, per usual, Dad checked in the rear-view mirror before he craned his neck over his shoulder. While backing up, he kept a steady hand on the wheel. If my mother or oldest sister were navigating this portion of the driveway, Dad always inhaled slightly, only softly exhaling when the car appeared intact on Hale Street. I had tried to erase the memory of my father from a year ago, when he'd not been able to drive after his nervous breakdown.

If Dad didn't ever bring it up, why would I?

Instead, I asked Dad why we called the headquarters for the family business The Other Place. "We never put it up for a vote," he said, shifting gears as we drove down Cabot Street. "It evolved naturally. Not home? Then we must be at The Other Place. The term stuck."

I grinned. It suited the brown clapboard house, tucked behind a brick factory, near the railroad tracks. We'd added a cement block storage and shipping plant. Rear Rantoul Street was too ugly to say out loud. And HQ was too formal. "The Other Place" felt descriptive of this modest commercial and residential facility hidden from the town's main drag.

By then, I realized Dad had eased into a parking spot, opening my door. We started up the stairs, as an older man touched Dad's sleeve. "Charlie Elliott! What a sight for sore eyes. How long since you've set foot at Sylvania? Years? Hey, that means your business must be doing A-OK." Turning toward me, he said, "Young lady, did you know your father was my supervisor? What a great guy to work for." My father deflected the compliment by introducing me. With a wink, the man said, "It's an honor to meet the daughter he named the company for." Should I curtsy? Opting for a less dramatic response, I giggled. "Nice meeting you, too."

While they wound up their chat, I thought about the Sylvania worker's comments. Having worked at the nearby shipping plant, I knew he was right. Dad respected his fellow workers. If Grace or Janet needed a day off for a personal reason, Dad always accommodated them. He was as kind at work as at home. I'd taken my father's sensitivity in the workplace for granted. Weren't all bosses as nice as Dad? Years later, in a variety of corporate positions, I realized Dad's high ethical standards and regard for his co-workers was the exception rather than the rule.

When this man mentioned Sylvania in Lynn, I had no point of reference. After all, in those days, I'd been a baby. My recollections began as a toddler with Dad peddling the huge linotype printing press in the basement. Over the next few years, as the business grew, he'd rented a variety of empty spaces in commercial buildings in North Beverly and Danvers. Long after our favorite TV shows and bedtime, we kids overheard our parents' voices whispering the pros and cons of purchasing a commercial building dedicated to the business. They finally agreed: To grow, they had to take a big risk. The packaging and shipping plant they envisioned from the run-down property at 50 Rear Rantoul Street would be a four-minute commute to downtown, even closer to the P.O. Eventually, the card company encompassed these places: the modest plant on the other side of town, the Hale Street colonial home that included: Mom's den office, the attic ping pong table groaning with Christmas Card albums, and the alcove behind Susan's bedroom containing metal filing cabinets. And, always, there was enough work for us, a handful of friends, as well as five part-time plant employees.

If we had tried calculating all the hours Mom and Dad worked, we would have thrown our hands up in defeat. There was no such thing as a traditional eight-hour day. Long after "the Shoe" blasted its five-p.m. siren, Mom and Dad had their heads together on a work-related task. Sure, they'd share a scotch before sitting down with us for dinner. After we did our homework, they'd enter orders in the thick, three-ring binders stored in the den closet. Weekends did not mean two days of relaxation. Saturday morning or Sunday evening, they'd study spread sheets or pour over the accounting books. I'd watch as they smiled or whooped over a surprisingly big order from a buyer at John Wanamaker's in Philadelphia.

Now, I wondered, what would Dad's life have been like if he'd managed to overcome the obstacles he'd outlined to become a golf pro? Dad's passion for golf had once motivated him to dig three makeshift golf holes around the yard at 57 Dane Street. "Slightly better than pitch and putt golf," he said under his breath. To my untrained eye, he was a natural. *Plunk!* The ball sank into the hole effortlessly, like a homing pigeon. When no one was looking, I grabbed a club. Swinging it, I watched the ball arc up in the air. Not bad! Less than a year later, in 1955, we filled in those holes in the yard before we moved to a more upscale section of town called Beverly Cove. Dad tucked away his bag of clubs in the barn to collect dust, an admission that the game was too demanding. He never complained. Instead, he buffed up his tennis skills and taught Mom to play the game. Eventually, his love for this sport got all four of us kids playing. I think he preferred sports that he could share with the whole family, not unlike the way we all shared the work in the family business.

After saying good-bye—without a curtsy—to Dad's former co-worker, we hiked up the steps of the post office. I enjoyed hopping up the stairs, two at a time, to keep up to Dad's long-legged stride. This imposing granite building spanned the entire block, fronting on Rantoul Street, the thoroughfare that connected North Beverly and Salem. At the turn of the century, the building's Classical Revival style must have impressed townspeople gazing at its expanse of granite steps mounting toward tall, Greek columns. The architect probably had not envisioned that by 1958, duplexes and triplexes would be its unappealing neighbors. Indeed, the hodgepodge of paint-peeling triple-deckers, pubs, and saloons made a sad contrast to its grand edifice. To me, it stood like a citadel amid the ruins at its feet.

Behind the wall of boxes lay a cavernous room containing a huge metal table surrounded by postal carriers. If I poked my face up close to Box 23, I could see beyond, back to those men working. Mostly, I heard their steady buzz of conversation. Before machines did the sorting, those workers spread the mail over the table to organize for the afternoon truck deliveries. Thanks to my father's P.O. connections, three years later, Bud would land a coveted, well-paying assignment there during his college holiday break. He had us all laughing one night at dinner when he recounted his supervisor's instructions in the back room.

"Hey smart asses, slow down! Are you trying to make us regulars look bad? Sort 'em all over again if you must. We don't hit the road to deliver the mail until the afternoon. So, take your sweet time in here. Understand, frat boys?" Bud slapped the table for emphasis, imitating his supervisor.

I'd never gain entrance to the long worktable and its team of regulars. They didn't hire young college women for those desirable holiday stints. Nevertheless, the P.O. seemed magical to me. After spinning through the twirling, brass turnstile, I'd land in the central hall, a huge, vaulted room resplendent in Vermont marble. The shiny floor had a patina from decades of patrons walking over it. One-person postal booths topped with wrought iron bars housed stamps, tape, boxes, and various shipping materials. The main attraction, however, was the wall of individual post office boxes. Each glass door twinkled, catching light from the high ceiling. Up close, I liked to trace my finger over the delicate gold fleur-de-lis in its corners. They sparkled as if atop a jewelry box.

That lucky morning when I was Dad's only companion, he nodded, as was his habit, to several other men in this room. They recognized each other, these regulars. This building must be a hangout, of sorts, a community gathering spot. Dad spent his weekdays at The Other Place, with a lunch break at home with Mom. Still, he popped in here frequently. He also made his Saturday stop here. I guessed that the P.O. was his *Other*, Other Place.

When we reached Box 23, I watched Dad turn the key in the door. *Click. Click.* The sound of metal against metal was magnified by the high ceiling as he opened the box. It was crammed full, like a Christmas gift. Hooray! Manila folders and piles of white and colored envelopes meant card orders and customer checks. I felt like doing an Irish jig.

I held out my arms so Dad could pile the spilling contents into them. Once back in the car, it would be my job to organize the hodgepodge. I hugged this treasure trove to my chest, watching Dad thrust his slight frame against the heavy door to let me exit first.

"Need help with that pile?" he asked.

I pursed my lips. "Dad, I've got it under control."

"Quite the gentleman," observed a man waiting outdoors on the granite landing. He was breathing heavily after his climb. A wispy circle of cigarette smoke wafted above his white hair. Waving it away with his scrawny arm, he repeated, "A real gent." That second compliment yielded a row of stained yellow teeth.

Dad said, "You'd do the same for your daughter. Her hands are full." Still, I knew that no matter the circumstances, my father would have adhered to the rules of etiquette: he opened doors, he pulled out a chair for you at the dinner table, he took your order first, because that's what a gentleman did.

Back inside the station wagon, I decided to bring up what had been on my mind, learning how to drive. I blurted, "Dad, are you going teach me to drive when it's my turn? When I turn sixteen?"

"Of course. I'm an old hand now. You know I taught your mother when we were dating. And you watched me teaching your older sister and brother. Just like Sue and Bud, you and Joan will learn on a stick shift. In an emergency, it's important that you're able to drive both a standard and a shift car."

Dad's preoccupation with worst case scenarios didn't get passed down genetically to us kids, thank goodness. Mom played a huge part in smoothing over his pessimism. Often, she kidded Dad out of his negative thoughts. Usually, she got him to laugh at himself. The exception had been the Williamsburg breakdown and Dad's subsequent recovery.

I didn't enjoy thinking about what had happened in Williamsburg. This morning, I preferred to congratulate myself for getting Dad on record committing to teach me to drive. He was a far better driver than Mom. As the youngest sibling, I was accustomed to waiting my turn. Top to bottom, with only four and a half years between us, taught me patience. Dad would have to teach me before declaring himself retired from his driving coach responsibility. Yay!

Meanwhile, I'd exhausted the driving conversation. Time to change the subject. I asked, "Hey, did you also teach Mom to play golf?"

"Absolutely. We went out on a public course or to a driving range, long before you were born. But she was never a fan. Too intense, time consuming. Tennis is more to her taste, especially the mixed doubles. It's fun playing with other couples."

I pressed my line of inquiry. "Dad, did you give golf lessons to Sue or Bud?" I must have sounded plaintive. He smiled. "Susan wasn't interested. The coup de grace was when she hit her close friend on the links at Mt. Holyoke College last fall."

How vividly I recalled Susan's chagrin when her errant ball hit Mary, an accomplished golfer. Undoubtedly, my sister's physical education elective had been made as a tip of the hat to Dad. She'd been willing to give his game a try. But after this mishap, Sue declared that her campus downtime would be better spent mastering bridge. Happily, it couldn't maim anyone.

"Bud? He was a whole different story," Dad continued, shifting into third as he anticipated the hill taking us to Nick's

Mobil gas station. "He's got the gift of hand-eye coordination. Remember how well he guarded shortstop in Little League? Well, 'good hands' and 'good eyes' are key to his favorite sports, basketball and tennis. That's why he caught on to golf quickly."

So why had Dad stopped with Bud? He had not invited Joan to the driving range or the links. How would he have reacted if I'd demonstrated hand and eye coordination? I was the family member who boasted superior long-distance vision.

"Look, Kristin, the business was growing. Golf takes time and money. Something had to give . . . and it was golf. Nothing overly complicated about that." Discussion over.

A well-kept secret surfaced almost fifty years later when my siblings and I collaborated on Dad's obituary. *The Boston Globe* writer pressed us all for anecdotes about him. That was when Bud offered memories of quitting early from The Other Place to play nine holes with Dad. We three sisters were nonplussed. According to my brother, it was one of the few times we were speechless. At close to ninety-one, Dad would have relished reading his own obit in the Irish sports pages of his beloved Boston newspaper.

But at thirteen, I knew nothing about secret golf outings between father and son. Oblivious to their shenanigans, it was all I could do to wrestle with the Box 23 bonanza of contents. Back in the car, they spilled down my lap to my sneakers.

Over breakfast, Dad had been excited reading about the newcomer to the PGA, Arnold Palmer. I wondered why, when Jack Nicklaus was the name who dominated the sport. Out of nowhere, I asked, "Why do you like Arnie Palmer?"

Without hesitation, Dad said, "Arnie plays quickly and efficiently. He's a perfect gentleman. Never shows a temper. Never wastes minutes lining up his putt. A no nonsense approach." As if reading my mind, he added, "Nicklaus takes his pretty time, deliberating, analyzing every blade of grass on the green. Arnie doesn't overthink it."

The way he talked about Arnie, he could have been describing himself. But Dad wasn't done. He tapped the wheel, keeping my attention.

"Remember: Golf is the game of life. In part, because it takes four hours to play. The back nine is the true test of character. That's when the body gets tired and the brain distracted. If a man shows anger by the fifteenth hole, beware. If he's shaving his score, that's a red flag. You might say that golf is a good test of a future husband."

Wow, okay. I was stunned. My father was offering husband advice, for heaven's sake. He'd never talked like this with me. Had being behind the wheel loosened his tongue? And, I didn't play golf. Gosh, I hadn't even been on an official date yet. Maybe I could substitute tennis for golf? I was beginning to show promise with a strong forehand and graceful backhand. But would his analogy still hold? I was guessing a clever man could disguise his character for one and a half hours on the court more successfully than four hours on the links.

"Dad, if golf is the test of a man's character—a man who wishes to be husband material—is there a second test, just in case?"

"Sure, right here. The next best test is driving a car," he said, gesturing toward the windshield. "Does he weave in and out of traffic? Run a red light? Swear at others on the road?" He wasn't kidding.

"Sounds a lot like golf." I laughed.

Dad chuckled. "Well, now that you mention it . . . ."

Once more, I realized that my introverted father met his own criteria and then some. He was an excellent driver, courteous yet defensive. I'd heard him swear, plenty, yet never behind the wheel. I'd been in the back seat of many friends' cars when their fathers were driving. There were plenty of *God damns!* Squealing of brakes. Obscene hand gestures.

Dad maneuvered the turn, pulling into the gas station by a pump. Nick grinned under the brim of his grease-stained Red Sox baseball cap, unscrewing the gas lid. He tipped his hat at me, mouthing a big *Hello, Kristin* to me. Dad popped out for a sports chat. Nick brought up Ted Williams, the team's bad boy, how he'd saved the day during the double header the previous night against the Sox archrival, the Yankees. *Ping! Ping!* A full tank. Reluctantly, they cut off their play-by-play of their Red Sox team. I waved good-bye out the cranked-down window as Dad turned the ignition key. Naturally, it caught, first time, as he eased out the clutch.

"Why do you overlook Ted Williams' temper?" I asked Dad. After all, he'd just lectured me about the virtue of keeping cool on the golf links. I was confused.

He cleared his throat. "In my opinion, Williams deserves being the exception to that rule. The press and some team fans vilify him. Consider the guy's phenomenal record, despite volunteering in combat missions, not once, but twice, in both World War II and the Korean War. He took a huge hit to his income—and career statistics—during those timeouts. He also risked his life flying dangerous air missions, a task he was given because of his superior vision. Despite all that, the fans jeer him."

For Dad, that came close to a speech. Like Williams, I had better than excellent eyesight. Dad rooted for underdogs and the Red Sox epitomized underdog status, holding their devoted fans in thrall throughout the season before letting them down in the fall. Right on the spot, I made an easy decision to be a Williams fan, too.

Boy, my father had been full of surprises during our morning run to the P.O. He'd shared two criteria for husband potential. Usually, he gave three reasons. Besides golf and driving a car, would the third test involve another activity? Like sex? It certainly was a vital force between him and Mom. But my teenaged mind did not want to picture them having sex.

I sighed as we swung into our driveway. Inside, Mom was still typing in her ladder-back chair by the den window. We'd only been away an hour. Why did it feel like more?

Years later, I would share Dad's husband criteria with friends and lovers. Dad's fatherly advice for a prospective mate was intimidating. No doubt, the ideal candidate for me to bring home would have been a hybrid of Arnie Palmer and Ted Williams.

Ages after Bud had played hooky to sneak out on a golf course with Dad, I took up the game. I'd always wished to find an activity I could share one on one with Dad, to have exclusive time with him. After college, I lived for a decade in New York City before eventually moving to suburban New Jersey where I had easy access to county courses. It was finally when I was in my early forties and Dad in his mid-seventies, that I flew home to Beverly to play a round of golf that he'd arranged.

My heart was racing at the first tee. Dad, semi-retired from Kristin Elliott, Inc., couldn't see well because he was facing cataract surgery. As he prepared for tee off, he said, "Describe what you see ahead, Kristin."

"Dad, this hole is a dog leg left, about 140 feet out."

Without fanfare, Dad stepped up, did a practice swing, and smacked the ball onto the fairway. Why was I not amazed that the ball landed where he'd aimed it? He called this talent muscle memory. With him, I became better at estimating distances and studying the lay of the land. To this day, I have no need for technological gadgets. He had not found time to take me out on the links as an adolescent, but he made up for it when we were adults.

After this first round, over cocktails, Mom asked how I'd performed. I held my breath as Dad volunteered. "Good thing she has a decent day job, Betsy." I tried not to show my disappointment. Mercifully, he added, "Actually, she's got potential." Coming from Dad, this critique felt like high praise. Throughout my forties and fifties, I pinched myself every time I got out on the links with my father.

Now, when I hit the ball long and straight, it's Dad voice that I hear in my ear, saying "nicely done." What a pleasure to have walked many courses with him, a gifted player who had turned his back on a youthful dream of becoming a pro.

I never did meet a prospective husband who passed the golf portion of the husband test. But it's no surprise that when I think about Dad, it's often on the golf course.

GETTING MY LICENSE

ONE SPRING AFTERNOON, while digging into a half-empty box of Cheez-its, I stared out the dining room window, analyzing the ridiculously tight space between our home and our neighbor's house. While crunching down on a salty orange square, I imagined this divide had been big enough for horses in the 1770s, but trickier for vehicles in the 1960s. The tunnel-like passageway had never bothered me when my father was behind the wheel, backing up, but it had taken on an ominous presence when my older siblings were learning how to drive. In a few minutes, it would be my turn. I especially didn't want to disappoint my father during our first driving lesson.

The family dynamic had shifted since Joan and I were now the only two living at home. With her driver license tucked inside her wallet, Joan had power. To persuade her to run an errand or drop me off at a friend's house, I resorted to wheedling. Or bribing, telling her she could wear my new Lantz dress, which I'd only worn once. I brushed orange crumbs from my palms over my dungarees. Time to grow up!

The grandfather clock chimed as I returned the Cheez-its box to the kitchen.

Always on time, Dad walked in the kitchen door, holding the contents of PO Box 23 in his arms. He shouted out his arrival. "Hello, Betsy! I'm home. Hello, Kristin. Let me check in with your mother."

Did he remember he'd had an appointment with me? I wondered. "Hey, Dad, you promised at breakfast that you'd start my driving lessons as soon as you got home from The Other Place today."

Dad gave me a faraway look and a faint smile.

Then he made a beeline for the den where Mom's steady typing gave away her whereabouts. His face revealed his eagerness to show her the generous pile of mail he'd picked up at the P.O. I was wishing I still had a few more Cheez-its to assuage my anxiety. Instead, I trailed into the den behind him.

He leaned over to plant a kiss on Mom's cheek. She looked up at both of us and must have seen impatience in my expression, weariness in his. "Charlie, you absolutely did promise. Drinks can wait. Scoot, both of you!"

Two against one. Mom was on my side. He was defeated. "Okay, grab the keys to the Saab on your way out, Kristin."

I thought back to our dinner conversation the night before. Joan had been boasting about how she'd parallel parked the car downtown, complimenting Dad on how well he'd taught her that maneuver. Then, Dad reminisced about his past coaching sessions, which began with Mom. We were familiar with this story because otherwise, Mom would never have been able to accept her job as a nutritionist for the Eastern States Farmers' Exchange.

Decades later, it seemed logical to our family that when each of us kids turned sixteen, he'd be our designated teacher. If Dad remembered those sessions as frustrating or frightening, he made no mention of them.

Over Mom's buttery biscuits, Dad recalled Susan's penchant for maintaining eye contact with backseat friends. "Despite her social inclinations, she passed the test," he said.

Bud? "Well, he had a bit of a heavy foot and an agile index finger that always landed on his favorite rock 'n' roll radio station. I heard a lot of Elvis and Ray Charles, but he caught on quickly."

Facing Joan, he cleared his throat. "Well, you did all right. Better at looking at the road than your older sister. Proof is in the pudding. Here you are, driving downtown and parking the car without a problem."

Joan grinned. I wondered if she slept with that license under her pillow. Privately, she'd confided that Dad gritted his teeth during some of their lessons. "He actually cringed when I backed up through the driveway between the two houses. I dreaded that passage to the street. I think he did, too."

As I buttered my biscuit, I thought about Dad's summary of our family driving lessons. He'd sounded like a man who had his eye on the finish line. Checking each kid off the list as another mission accomplished. Three down (not counting Mom, of course), one to go. As if hearing my inner thoughts, Dad said, "Only one more Elliott to go!"

Now, this afternoon, ever the man of manners, Dad escorted me to the driver's side of the small car. He got in next to me and pulled his door shut, firmly. Since I usually sat in that seat, I knew the pesky door had a mind of its own. Two attempts to shut and secure it were not uncommon, but he succeeded on his first try. One of my sister's chubby girlfriends refused to sit in that seat.

After turning on the ignition, I faced Dad. He reached over me and turned it off.

"Oh no! What now?" I wondered. I thought back to my enrollment in after-school Drivers Education. The nervous instructor had pumped his brake over and over in our specially equipped car. Was I hard of hearing? Hadn't he asked me to stop? I didn't think his questions deserved an answer, and he didn't seem to expect one. Our frustrating exchange was only the beginning of a series of odd lesson plans. Dizzying circles followed long turns in the empty lot behind Beverly High School. One afternoon, he directed me a half-mile away to the corporate campus of the United Shoe Machinery Company. There, side roads and parking lots provided a quiet tableau without real world driving distractions: a fantasy world with no pedestrians, traffic lights, speeding cars, rumbling trucks, hidden potholes, honking horns, or blind corners. This teacher, I guessed, had one goal: to outlive generations of teenage drivers. And right then, I was smack in his way, making him wonder if he'd reach retirement and his pension.

How would these elementary turns, stops, and starts prepare me for a demanding road test with its legendary criteria: parallel parking, stopping on a steep hill, and at least one left-hand turn? My instructor patted me on the shoulder when our sessions were over. "Don't be such a worrywart, Kristin. You'll do fine when the time comes." Little did he know that I was the designated worrywart in our family, superseded only by my father.

So here I was, sitting next to Dad, in this quirky car. Why couldn't we have a normal car like everyone else? But Mom and Dad had made a practical decision after Bud went away to Williams College, turning in her four-door turquoise Pontiac convertible for a two-door compact GT750 Saab. They'd been won over by the Swedish car's abbreviated size, appropriate for running errands downtown. Mom in particular was a fan of its newest innovation, seat belts. For them, practicality superseded glamour. Almost two years later, Joan and I still mourned the loss of her snazzy convertible. We were pretty sure Mom missed it, too.

A selling point at the Saab dealership had been that the vehicle technology was based on the Swedish company's airplane engine expertise. What, I wondered, did airplane design have to do with an automobile? The odd, bottle-shaped black car made almost as much noise as a Boeing jet leaving the runway when we tooled around Beverly, waving to friends.

"Here come the Elliott girls in their ground-level version of a plane," classmates teased us. More than once, the car spluttered at an intersection. Was it something to do with takeoff? Landing? We never found a car mechanic to explain the eccentricities of its engine. Fortunately, traffic was modest in 1962 in our Boston suburb.

Now Dad put his hand over mine as I reached to turn on the ignition. He pulled my hand back with his. "Before we tackle the driveway, let's consider all five gears. And, of course, the clutch. It's critical not to burn it out when switching gears." He demonstrated where the gears were located. I'd already learned about them from my school instructor. Nevertheless, it had more gravitas coming from my dad and while in Mom's car, not the special car with two brakes. I frowned, then nodded to indicate an understanding that I wasn't sure of. Only then did I turn the key in the ignition.

Vroom! Bombs away! Blast off! Through the rear window, I saw puffs of black. My nose scrunched up, inhaling whatever the stuff was coming out of the tailpipe.

I shifted into reverse and paused. Dad once again placed his large hand over mine. He reminded me to always adjust the rear-view mirror to my height and to check for imaginary moving vehicles and pedestrians.

"Look right, then left, and behind before allowing the car to move. Drive conservatively. Assume the worst," he said. This snippet of wisdom fit Dad's Irish outlook on life, just like his belief that I'd be the person who knew how to drive a stick shift in a situation when that mode of transportation was the one and only way to save someone's life.

I looked over at Dad. Was he going finally going to let me shift into reverse? His eyes closed briefly, then re-opened. Slowly, I backed up. The car stuttered. Belatedly, Dad, not a fan of seat belts, grabbed his and snapped it around his thin torso. *Click!*

Herkily, jerkily, we made our way toward the narrowest stretch of driveway. "Do your best not to hit either of these venerable homes," he said dryly. "They're American treasures that have survived almost 200 years of horses and buggies. Why alter history now?" He chuckled, pleased with his humor.

With Dad still smiling, I cautiously navigated through our home-grown version of the Strait of Magellan until I reached my goal: the sidewalk. We'd not risk the heavily trafficked Hale Street on our first foray. No, siree! I sniffed the smoke billowing from the tailpipe. "Okay, then. You didn't hit the neighbor's house. Off to a decent start. Put the car into first gear, slowly go into second, and pull up by the barn. For this afternoon, your lesson is complete."

Complete, as in . . . over? Really?

I hadn't been around to calculate the length of my siblings' first lessons with Dad, but I was willing to bet that mine set a record for the shortest in length. From settling in behind the wheel, to braking by the barn door, it had taken only twenty minutes.

"Good going. Time to relax and enjoy my scotch with your mother," Dad said.

I asked myself where the "born teacher" had gone, the man with the patience of Job, Mom's description when fondly recalling her lessons with him.

Didn't class usually last one hour? Especially the first? Had my father cut mine short because it delayed his favorite daily ritual, drinking cocktails while trading stories about Kristin Elliott, Inc.? Certainly, I didn't want to consider that Dad had run out of steam after four years of teaching my siblings. How could my skills be worse than Susan's, Bud's, or Joan's? After all, I was the only one of us with better than perfect vision.

Opening the screen door, Dad shouted, "Class over! We survived getting down the driveway and as far as the street. I'm making myself a double scotch!"

During dinner that night, Dad cleared his throat. He announced that over the next few weeks, the business would be pressed with large orders for Wanamaker's in Philadelphia and Miller and Rhodes in Richmond. And, he added, his plant employee, Gerry, needed a short time off.

"Betsy, would you take over the teaching job for Kristin?" Tears sprang to my eyes. Mom hid her surprise by swallowing a gulp of water. All of us knew how impatient a teacher she was.

In her role as cook, she preferred we learn by observation rather than as sous chefs. That model of teaching would not carry over well from the kitchen to a compact vehicle.

"Of course, Charlie. I'll have her driving like a pro in no time." I caught Joan's eye. She shrugged. We both knew a decision had been made.

Over the next weeks, Mom sat with clenched fists as I backed out into Hale Street traffic, bucked uphill on Prospect Street, and screeched to a stop. Sometimes, there was telltale smoke spewing from the tailpipe. I felt like the East Coast version of a Texas cowgirl busting a bronco. Mom muttered, "How did your father do this, not once, twice, but three times? Well, four actually, counting me."

We covered all the criteria for the test, repeatedly. The car began to smoke less and respond to my touch. Mom, eager to return to her typewriter, pronounced that I was ready and should initiate the required agency tests.

In the long-tiled corridors of Beverly High, as green metal locker doors slammed shut, I'd heard the gossip about driving tests scheduled and flunked. Some classmates kept their test dates secret because it wasn't uncommon to come out of the agency empty-handed. Was it a power trip for those test givers who had the ability to pass or fail young drivers? Whatever it was, no one was super cocky walking in for an appointment.

After overstudying the manual, I took the written exam . . . and passed with flying colors. Wahoo! That was the easy part. My critical date for the road test required an adult with a valid license accompany me in the car. The test was scheduled on a weekday afternoon. Mom was my logical companion.

We drove downtown to the driving agency, Mom at the wheel. Surprisingly, she found a parking spot in front of the glass front doors right away. "Our good luck!" she exclaimed. "This bodes well for you."

"Mom, I'll go in and find the tester. In the interim, why don't you pop into the back seat?" Mom smiled demurely as she rearranged her silk scarf and puffed up her hair. Then, she prepared to tuck herself neatly behind the passenger seat.

"Oh, Mom, just one favor. I'm feeling a bit nervous. Don't tell me not to be, please! It would be great if during the test you simply said nothing. Maybe 'hello' and 'goodbye?' Nothing else. Got it?"

Mom's smile vanished. "Of course, if that's what you wish. I can't imagine why I have to be silent. But you're in the driver's seat." She giggled.

"Whew. Thanks, Mom. I appreciate it."

I pushed through the agency front door, heart pounding. Hey, this wasn't rocket science. Everyone in the world had a license, for heaven's sake. At the lobby, I was waved past beige walls and dull linoleum floors toward rows of cubicles. From one emerged an oversized man. He lumbered toward me. Was that the floor, shuddering under his bulk? Obviously, he was my "thumbs up" or "thumbs down" guy. His soiled white shirt (pizza for lunch?) struggled to free itself from his trousers, belted below his bulging belly. Despite air-conditioning, he was sweating. When he stopped his trek in front of me, I smelled onions. I could feel resentment radiating off his florid face.

"Miss Elliott?" I nodded, afraid to speak. "Good thing you're on time. You are my last appointment of the day." He raised both hands and gestured toward the lobby. "Go out the way you came in."

Outdoors, I got into the car behind the wheel, fastening my belt. I carefully adjusted the mirror. Gazing into it, I spied Mom with her wide eyes growing wider as the new occupant plunged into the seat before her. She was tut-tutting her disapproval. I crossed my fingers that he could not hear her. His fleshy hands grabbed the door handle to pull it shut. Of course, the door did not cooperate. He grabbed the door handle harder. *Whoosh! Whoosh!* Still, a no go. His fourth and final effort was a yank that almost unhinged the door. Now, his flushed face was redder. He slowly wiped the sweat from his forehead, wiping it on his wrinkled shirt. Then he had a staring contest with his seat belt. Could it expand to make the journey over his waist? He sighed, dropping the offending belt.

His mouth curled with distaste. "Hate these buggers. Made to torture."

Behind him, in her cave-like space, my mother spoke, "My, aren't you a large man for such a little car?"

I sank lower behind the wheel. What had I begged her not to do? He made an effort to get a good look at her, but his girth did not allow it. His upper body was imprisoned into a front-facing position, spilling dangerously close to the gear shift. I longed for the Pontiac, with its wide front seat and four doors. So much more accommodating! Belatedly, I introduced him to the disembodied voice of the Queen of England in the back seat. My final adjustment? The rearview mirror, a second time. Dad would have been proud of me. I made sure to angle it, blocking the sight of Mom's smirk.

"Well, what are you waiting for?" he said. "By the way, what kind of car is this? Not American, you can't fool me. I also see it has no air-conditioner." As he wiped his forehead with a damp hanky, I resisted telling him that my parents thought A/C in a town on the ocean was superfluous. And that foreign manufacturers were beginning to compete with American car makers.

None of this information would have helped my cause. Quite the opposite.

"Okay, kid. Pull out on Cabot Street, here. Let's get this over with," he said.

I put my hand out to signal and entered the traffic, shifting from first to second. Yay, no stripping of gears. "Make a right off Cabot. Now!" I navigated the turn smoothly. When would he issue the dreaded left-hand command, now that we were in late afternoon traffic? He repeated, "Right, again!" Once more, I did his bidding. We were bypassing the steep hill at Prospect Street that all test takers had to endure. "One more right, Miss." Now, I was upset. It didn't take a math genius to know that three right hand turns were bringing us directly back to our point of origin. No left turn, no stopping or starting on a hill, no parallel parking. I'd never gotten to fourth gear. It was too easy. It wasn't taking enough time and reminded me of my one and only lesson with Dad. Had I flunked without being given a fair chance, because he, too, was eager to end his day?

"Okay, pull over there," he said. I swerved the car into the space we'd vacated minutes ago.

"Why are we back so fast?" I asked. He glared at me.

"You're still some distance from the curb. Pull in, like I directed you. To really park this so-called car." I meekly complied, realizing I'd given him a bona fide reason to fail me. Damn!

Click! I unfastened my seat belt as his car door sprang open, scraping the sidewalk. *Screech! Scrunch!* Slowly, he hoisted himself up and out of the seat, groaning as he stood. I tried not to stare at the spectacle. Once he was standing on the sidewalk, the car sprang back to its normal height. He left the offending door open, presumably so Mom could climb out. I followed him into the bowels of the agency, clutching the car keys, holding back tears.

When we got to his desk, he said, "Look, I'm passing you. I need to get the hell home. What I don't need? To be driving around town in a crap car that could kill me. Consider yourself lucky, kid, that I'm in a good mood." My body was trembling. This was his good mood? No matter, he'd said the magic words. I had passed. How ridiculous! Even so, I knew this story would be fun in the re-telling.

I strode out, temporary license in hand. My badge of courage! Mom was positioned in the passenger seat. She leaned out the open window with a smug expression. "Congrats! I knew you would pass, honey. Why were you so nerved up? Don't you agree that I deserve a huge pat on the back for being such a good teacher?"

ON THE CAMPAIGN TRAIL

This is good old Boston,
The home of the bean and the cod,
Where the Lowells talk to the Cabots
And the Cabots talk only to God.

THIS BOSTON DITTY dates back to the early 1900s, but was still floating about when I was growing up, especially because Beverly had its own Cabot, Henry Cabot Lodge, Jr. As the head of a political dynasty of wealthy Yankees, he lived on a compound secluded from the road and visible only by boat. Old money, after all, in New England, is discreet.

In that post-World War II era of prosperity and growth, Republicans rode a big wave of political popularity, led by the country's biggest war hero, President Dwight D. Eisenhower. Even my blue-collar town embraced the Eisenhower/Nixon ticket in 1952 and again in 1956.

By 1960, my parents still considered themselves liberal Republicans. They pointed out to us that there were not many policy differences between them and moderate Democrats. Still, if you told my parents that when Lyndon Baines Johnson faced off against Barry Goldwater in 1964, they'd be pulling the Democratic lever, they'd have been surprised. Looking back, I thought that their political evolution was amazingly progressive, more so as they aged. My father had never been a fan of Richard Nixon whom he unfailingly referred to as "Tricky Dick." Dad despised Nixon's Communist-baiting campaign to win his California Senate seat as early as 1950, when he accused his opponent, Helen Gahagan Douglas, of being a Pink Lady Communist, "pink right down to her underwear."

"Tricky Dick is a sexist bully," Dad said, "tapping into McCarthyism to bolster his political ambitions." The comment hit home with me. Wasn't his histrionic attack on Senator Douglas similar to the goings-on during the Salem witch trials, when powerful men channeled public fear against women and girls?

As the political turmoil of the 1960s unfolded, my parents were admirers of Martin Luther King and the Civil Rights Movement. Like my generation, they became staunch opponents of the Vietnam War. The last straw was when the Republican Party nominated for president the conservative Senator from Arizona, Barry Goldwater. Their defection to the Democratic party seemed like a natural step.

But my parents' political movement from the middle to the left still lay ahead. In 1960, Beverly and most of its citizens, went apoplectic when Nixon tapped Henry Cabot Lodge, Jr., as his Vice President. My father complained, "Just because Nixon tapped a man of Lodge's stature to be his Number Two doesn't redeem him in my eyes. The ticket should be reversed." Dad said out loud what almost everyone we knew was thinking: Lodge was the man who deserved to be at the top of the ticket, with Nixon under him.

One of Lodge's first rallies after the summer Republican Convention in Chicago was held on the Beverly Commons in front of Hardie School. Standing on tiptoe, I could barely make out the local and state politicians seated on the temporary stage erected in front of my former grammar school. Each was jostling to enhance his status by being on the dais with the national VP nominee. Only fourteen, I had little political motivation for showing up. I wanted to see our famous native son in the flesh! Of course, I'd seen pictures of his handsome, chiseled face in the *Globe* and the *Herald*, the two rival Boston newspapers. And I'd watched news snippets of him talking about Massachusetts issues on the CBS News at night. But seeing him without a media filter would be historic. The undercurrent of this crowd echoed what Dad had declared over dinner, "This ticket is upside down." It was a good thing for Nixon that he hadn't come to Beverly to campaign with his running mate.

An elderly woman blocking my view poked her friend in the ribs. "Did I mention that I passed Cabot a hymnal at St. Peter's? It was the Sunday before he went out to the Chicago Republican convention, less than a month ago." She drew herself taller, making my ability to see what was on stage even more challenging. Lately, rumors were circulating that the sparsely attended Episcopal church was suddenly boasting standing-room only attendance. I guessed its numbers would swell during the campaign, yet doubted Henry Cabot Lodge would be around town much to go to church services.

Perhaps no one should be blamed for wanting to catch a close view of this distinguished public servant, I concluded. In 1952, he'd sacrificed his own Massachusetts Senate seat (to none other than John Fitzgerald Kennedy) when he led Eisenhower's presidential election campaign. His "all in" for

Eisenhower caused him to neglect his own race. To acknowledge his loyalty, Eisenhower appointed him Ambassador to the United Nations. Being the Veep pick would put him back in the political fray. Once again, he was facing off against his rival, John F. Kennedy. Ironically, the much younger Kennedy was on the top of the Democratic presidential ticket.

In this election, it was juicy material for journalists to be able to cover two venerable Massachusetts families—the Democratic Kennedys and the Republican Lodges—as they battled their philosophical differences. The contrast between Lodge, the older, patrician politician, and his much younger, brash opponent was a photographer's dream assignment. These images sold newspapers and persuaded viewers to turn on their television sets.

On that day of the Lodge rally, as I craned my neck to see the candidate, I felt a heel crunch down on my big toe. The tall woman in front of me had stepped back onto my penny loafers. Had I been listening to the speeches that droned on and on and caused the microphone to squeak and screech at times? Do I remember what Lodge said that afternoon? No. But it occurred to me that, unlike what the little ditty said, this Cabot Lodge, straight out of Central Casting (Gary Cooper could play him in a movie) was speaking to a wider audience: Potential voters beyond our small town. As he spoke, he flashed an engaging smile. What a contrast to his running mate, Richard M. Nixon.

As I recounted my admiration for Lodge over the dinner table, Dad said, "Don't forget, he puts his pants on like every other man. Famous people are no different from the rest of us. As F. Scott Fitzgerald said about the wealthy: 'They simply have more money.' What matters is what they do with their skills and talents. If you're still awestruck in their presence, picture them nude. That levels the playing field."

I cackled, suppressing a snort. Happily, his advice still works for me.

The press reported that any reception at the Lodge mansion was a spartan event, with no leftovers. According to their reports, Emily Lodge's thrifty offerings consisted of store-bought Hydrox cookies and tepid Salada tea. This underwhelming menu underlined that the Lodges were a family of old money. As we all knew, Boston Brahmins did not flaunt their wealth. Had Dad been running for office (a difficult scenario for me to imagine), my mother would have baked plenty of Toll House cookies and moist brownies and brewed home-made iced tea. She'd have been generous! For that matter, I was pretty sure that Jackie Kennedy's receptions would be handsomely catered. Undoubtedly, a few guests—and even the press—might surreptitiously pocket a treat or two on their way out.

That day, the rally marked the origins of my engagement with politics. Like the masses, I was curious about this imposing politician who'd lost his Senate seat to the "whippersnapper," as Republican pundits referred to the young John F. Kennedy. Sure, I'd seen Lodge on television, on the front cover of *Time* magazine, and of course in black and white photographs in *The Boston Globe*. But I'd yet to meet an elected state or national politician. What lingered after the crowd had dispersed? A sense of excitement, a sense of pride that Beverly had put itself on the national map.

Fast forward to 1962, when Cabot Lodge's son, George Cabot Lodge, became the Republican nominee for the Massachusetts Senate in a special election created by JFK's vacant Senate seat. Running against Lodge in the primary was an older, conservative Republican who no one paid attention to. However, the two Democratic candidates who were pitted against each other were eye candy for the media: Edward McCormack—nephew of the U.S. Speaker of the House—and Ted Kennedy—JFK's youngest brother. The reporters were swooning . . . not one, not two, but three good-looking men in their thirties (Ted had just turned thirty, the minimum legal age to run for this office), all from famous Massachusetts families.

Joan and I were eager to learn how a U.S. Senate race operated at the grass roots level. Off she'd go to Mt. Holyoke in the fall, eventually to major in political science as our sister Susan had. Me? I'd continue my routine at home as a senior at Beverly High. I proposed writing a feature article for the Beverly High School literary magazine, the *Aegis*, and got the assignment. Move over, I wanted to say to historian Theodore H. White with his best-selling book, *The Making of the President 1960*! By working on the 1962 campaign trail with candidate George Cabot Lodge, I'd have an even better inside story. Together, my sister and I volunteered for Lodge's campaign, knowing that our benevolent boss, our father, would agree to the occasional day off from Kristin Elliott, Inc.

We'd drive the *putt, putt, putting* Saab to a metro station west of Boston off Route 128, beating the early morning commuter traffic. There, the campaign buses convened, awaiting youth volunteers and a variety of other non-paid local staffers. Throughout the day, we'd distribute flyers while our candidate shook hands, hands, and more hands. He'd greet Lowell mill workers filing in to punch their work cards, address a ladies' luncheon in Braintree, meet Polaroid Corporation employees leaving their sleek office complex in Waltham, and then go on to an evening rally in Framingham. The campaign trail wasn't glamorous at all, I decided. It started early and ended late. My feet were sore. I could only imagine how Lodge's arches flattened and how his palms ached.

Often, the three "Lodge for U.S. Senate" buses would create a backdrop for a spontaneous stage at a large shopping mall. From a megaphone, a voice would boom, "Come join us for an informal question-and-answer forum. Ask your next Massachusetts Senator what's on your mind!" Curious shoppers would meander over, as many as seventy or eighty. One question might be about Yugoslavia. Another about birth control or abortion. George Lodge would smile and answer the voters' many questions with grace and patience.

"Isn't he terrific?" Joan said. I'd nod, making a note in my omnipresent reporter's lined notepad to quote a line or two for my upcoming magazine feature. I was going to have a hard time keeping my essay to a manageable length.

I added, "Have you noticed how once in a while he hesitates before he answers? How he has a hard time getting out certain words? Usually late in the day?" When I'd been in grade school, my friend, Bert, who stuttered, took me with him to Boston for a speech pathology lesson. That experience had made an impression on me because Bert worked hours to manage his impediment. Stuttering also plagued Lodge, who almost always covered it up unless he was exhausted. His control was so good that the press ignored it. For me, it humanized him. No need to picture him nude.

Supper was late on campaign nights, leftovers warmed up. Mom would sit at the trestle table, with her chin cupped in her hands, listening to our stories. The days that she needed the Saab, Dad drove us over and picked us up for the forty-five minute commute to the campaign buses, if we couldn't carpool with another volunteer from the North Shore. It never occurred to me that we were inconveniencing our parents. I took it for granted that they'd be spellbound by our travels with the campaign.

Late on an August day, George Lodge approached Joan and me. "I know you're both Beverly girls. Turns out that I have room in a private car taking me home this evening. May I drop you off en route?"

I stared at my flats, not daring to look at Joan in case she was wearing her shit-eating grin. We had no need to huddle. "Wow, of course! That would be wonderful!" We were talking over one another in our excitement. As he returned to his staffer, Joan and I burst out laughing.

Joan said, "Yay! I know his address is in the high 200s on Hale Street. We live at 176 Hale. That's plus or minus a hundred houses. Not a big inconvenience."

I thought about what a difference there was in those one hundred houses. Ours was an even number on the wrong side of Hale Street while his home sat on the preferred side that stretched down to the ocean. His estate boasted a long driveway protected by shady trees that ended at a mansion and outer buildings that had breathtaking ocean views of Marblehead and Bakers Island. Our driveway? It was the infamous "tunnel," defined by two homes far too close to one another. Our view? A jam-packed, two-lane winding road filled with summer tourists taking the picturesque alternative to Route 128 in order to catch the ocean views through Beverly Farms, Manchester, Magnolia, Gloucester, and eventually, to Rockport.

"Listen, I'll find a pay phone to let Mom and Dad know that George offered to drop us off at our house," Joan said.

"After the rally, let's meet under that oak tree where he said he'd come looking for us."

It was dark by the time we stood under the designated tree, watching George politely extricate himself from the last few voters. I whispered to Joan, "Did you notice George stuttering a bit?"

"Yes. Guess it's because he's dragging. Bet he's glad this day is officially over."

"Me, too. And I'm not shaking hands all day long." We laughed, revved up for the drive home.

A black sedan pulled up next to us, a middle-aged man with salt and pepper hair behind the wheel. He popped out and held open the back door of the car, inviting Joan and me inside. A gentleman like Dad, I mused, gathering my skirt around my legs. I noted he wasn't wearing a chauffeur's uniform. Rather, he wore a tailored, pin-striped suit with a pressed white shirt and blue silk tie. When George Lodge appeared, I realized this tall man was his father.

"Hey . . . Dad, glad you're around for a couple days. And that you could . . . change your crazy schedule to pick me up. We'll have a chance to talk."

The father and son, both well over six feet, shook hands. I noted they were typical New England men, not hugging or embracing. And, not unlike Dad and Bud.

Henry Cabot Lodge, or "Cabot," as he was referred to in our town, was driving us home. I pinched myself. Even from the back seat, I could see he was breathtakingly handsome with crinkles around his bright eyes and a few lines accentuating his tanned cheeks. Joan and I squeezed each other's hands hard. George made quick introductions as his father put the car in drive.

143

Only fifty minutes to Beverly. Why couldn't it be hours?

The two politicians conversed the entire trip home. Even though they kept their voices low, we heard references to Teddy and the Kennedy family. The father asked the son about the enthusiasm of the crowds, and we strained to hear George's reply, but it was something like "they could be bigger." We both knew that after winning the primary in the race against the president's brother, George would be the underdog. But we were a family that cheered for the underdog. Both Joan and I kept our chatter to a minimum, eavesdropping the entire way. Clearly, these two men were not giving away any political secrets.

I watched their interaction. Once in a while, Cabot Lodge turned his son's way. Mostly, he kept his eyes on the road. Close to the Beverly exit on Brimbal Avenue, George stuttered. Joan caught my eye. I hugged my arms over my knees, feeling sorry for him.

That's when Cabot Lodge patted George's shoulder. As if on signal, George stopped mid-sentence. He paused for what felt like a long time. Then, George continued in a rush of words. "Let's not forget to drop off the terrific Elliott girls, Dad." George shifted around to us, revealing a crooked smile and eyes that were bloodshot, probably from exhaustion.

Our illustrious driver stopped directly in front of our colonial clapboard house. On cue, Mom and Dad opened the red front door. As they approached the car, I imagined I could hear them both take in a breath. Somewhere between the stone stoop and the sidewalk, they must have realized that our car held more than one Lodge.

Both Lodges stepped outside the car to greet my mother and father. They were not only politicians, but they were also courteous Beverly Cove neighbors. Suddenly, four pairs of adult hands reached out while making introductions. Pleasantries were exchanged. "Aren't you thoughtful to bring Joan and Kristin home with you." "Such a pleasure to meet you both!" "We're so glad you're running," aimed at the younger Lodge. And, of course, directed to the senior Lodge, "Thank you for your past service."

Then, the father and son got back into their car, and the car doors slammed shut. The four-door sedan whisked away. We stood outside, hugging, staring down the dark street at the rear red lights until we could no longer see them.

"Okay, nothing can top this moment," I said.

Joan said, "I will never, ever forget it."

Mom and Dad were grinning.

Like any cub reporter, I was celebrating. I'd gotten my scoop. I had an ending that I couldn't ever have dreamed of. I knew that I'd relish writing my article and feel proud when I saw it in print.

But my political Cinderella story wasn't complete. Something else one-upped this event. There was a second deadline besides that of my fall *Aegis* essay. A week later, Joan left for her freshman year at Mt. Holyoke.

I couldn't bear not seeing her off, not being part of this family milestone. My parents acquiesced. That morning, I showed up at Beverly High School. An hour later, I faked illness to be excused and sent home to bed.

As I plunked down in the station wagon idling outside the high school, Mom and Dad mentioned a last-minute detour to the polls to vote in the September primary. They worried voting might be over by the time we returned from the trip to South Hadley. All four of us peeled from the car. Joan and I waited as

Mom and Dad signed the forms and stood in the robust line of voters. The dueling Democrats and the local Republican aristocracy had created interest in this unusual early September primary. Suddenly, everyone was staring at the door. Like royalty, George and his wife, Nancy, came into the room. Over the length of the warped wooden floor, George spotted us. In seconds, his long legs spanned the room.

Flashlights popped. *Click, click!* Reporter's notebooks and sharpened pencils came out. "What a wonderful coincidence! Your daughters gave my campaign a great lift," George said.

Mom and Dad beamed. "Wonderful. Nice to see you again. We were thrilled they could have the experience." This ten-minute detour turned into a twenty-minute one. Coincidence? Or fortunate timing?

Was it hard saying good-bye on College Day One to Joan? You bet. But she was quickly ensconced, once she met her roommate, Marty. Together, they grappled with the challenge of fitting too much ugly furniture into a cramped dorm double. That was our signal to take off.

Coming home, my parents and I didn't talk much. It had been an emotional day from the moment Mom had snapped up my bedroom shades, announcing it was "Time to get up!"

Dad took the earlier Beverly exit, Ryal Side, off 128 because it was closer to the P.O. "I'd like to check PO Box 23. And grab a newspaper at Borah's shop across the street."

Mom closed her eyes briefly before she emitted a big sigh. I wondered if she was thinking, "Three down, one to go."

In a few minutes, Dad was opening his car door, laughing. He passed the *Beverly Evening Times* to Mom. "I bought three copies. You'll see why after you check out the front page, top

146

of the centerfold, where the big stories land." His index finger tapped the feature and accompanying photograph.

Mom's eyes widened. She giggled as she passed it over to me in the back.

"Hey, you can't get away with anything in this town," Dad said, still chuckling.

Much to my amazement, there was George Cabot Lodge, shaking hands with my parents. Joan and I were clearly recognizable behind them. So much for my cover story of feeling ill to the point that I'd had to leave school to go home to bed.

Was it possible to feel a little guilty and a lot lucky? That day, luck triumphed.

ACCEPTANCE

HOW OLD WAS I when I first heard the amazing story of how Dad underwent a vasectomy just after I'd been born? Mom and Dad explained that this method of birth control was safer and easier for men, compared to the more invasive procedure of women having their tubes tied. Dad pulled down his frayed copy of *Gray's Anatomy*, which he'd kept since his Harvard Medical School days, to show me the diagrams of men's and women's reproductive systems. I was sure my flushed cheeks gave away my embarrassment. I'm guessing I was in the sixth grade.

I felt relieved to have squeezed into this boisterous family, not unlike a Red Sox player stealing home from third base. As the youngest, my childhood mantra was basic: Keep up with the others! Wait for me! Deep down, I also wondered, How can I get attention on my own?

By seventeen, I was mature enough to acknowledge that my father's decision to take the birth control initiative had been unusual. In 1945, only a minute number of men would have considered being the spouse to assume responsibility. (Decades later, when I was part of the women's reproductive health team in Big Pharma, we joked that if birth control were left to men in America, we'd have to package it inside pizza!) When I first learned, at age eleven, how my parents faced this issue, I'd squirmed. The idea of the snip, snipping, close to the penis, in a doctor's office, seemed like information overload. Yikes! But as a teenager, Dad's decision felt bold. My parents had always been independent thinkers, starting with their decision to create the Kristin Elliott Christmas Card line. My mother had been an equal partner to my father while still earning kudos as an exemplary homemaker in an era when the majority of women did not have a career. Their agreement for Dad to undergo the snipping was yet another decision that was outside the mainstream.

When I considered what to write about in my college essay, I toyed briefly with the idea of Dad's pioneering decision, but I immediately discarded it. This essay was supposed to challenge me to describe how I could be a worthwhile member of a college community. A better idea, I decided, would be to write about my recent campaign experience with George Cabot Lodge, who had easily won the primary only to lose to Teddy Kennedy in the general election. But how I admired his hard work and commitment.

What, if anything, had I contributed to my family, to my high school class, or to my hometown during my adolescence? As first, Susan got the spotlight. As second, close behind her, Bud got the "only boy" attention. With Joan, it was a different story. She was always just one year ahead. To me, it felt like that gave her the edge. When my parents enrolled us in lessons to learn to play a musical instrument, we rented a flute that we shared. Neither of us practiced enough, but she mastered the instrument more easily than I did. After Saturday morning lessons at Edwards School near The Other Place, our teacher, Mr. Simonsson, would say to my father when he picked us up, "Joan reads the music well. Now, Kristin . . ." he paused, probably wanting our classes to continue throughout our high school years. "Hmm. Kristin has great breath control." I wondered if that talent might be more appropriate for a long-distance runner than an aspiring member of the woodwind section in band and orchestra.

Because my shyness lingered, I was less popular with boys than Joan. When she confided that Norman, a quiet guy with a hesitant smile who played clarinet a row behind us, had a crush on me, I was thrilled because he was nice. Unfortunately, he was shyer than I was, so we were tongue-tied over the span of three dates.

Secretly, I wished to excel in one activity of my own. Susan never met a test she didn't ace. Not surprisingly, she usually got all the answers right. Worse, she enjoyed replaying their content in detail afterwards. Bud, resembling the original Boy Scout with his *Father Knows Best* whiffle haircut and freckles, produced *ooh*'s and *ah*'s, with slick jackknife dives off the highest board on the wooden pier at West Beach. Mom liked flirting with his basketball buddies who dropped by to shoot hoops against our barn door. I admired Bud's athleticism, while harboring crushes on his good friends, Jeff and Gordie.

But how could I differentiate from Joan, whose world overlapped mine? Of course, she passed the Scholarship Key to me onstage during her Briscoe Junior High School graduation with both of us looking serious, wearing our pageboy flip haircuts and headbands. Over the next two years, I marched beside her in my woolen band uniform playing the flute or piccolo. I even joined the high school's *Aegis* literary magazine when she was an editor. I didn't know then what I do today: writing would be my calling, for my career and my retirement.

Was anyone surprised when Joan followed Susan's lead and chose Mt. Holyoke? Susan loved college and was elected to Junior Phi Beta Kappa. Two weeks after her 1962 graduation, she married in our backyard with each of us siblings playing roles in her intimate wedding. Joan entered college the next fall. Mt. Holyoke had been Mom's first choice twenty-five years earlier, before the Depression got in her way of being able to afford it. Needless to say, she was thrilled when both Susan and Joan opted to go there. It was even sweeter that Mt. Holyoke offered scholarship assistance.

At our high school, there weren't a lot of college prep students. Some classmates would not go on after graduation from Beverly High. Others elected to go to technical school after a major in vocational education. Of the college prep students, the majority went to nearby junior colleges or state schools like Salem State Teachers College and the University of Massachusetts. We had no advanced placement classes in the early 1960s. Instead, in hopes of better preparing ourselves for college, a handful of us elected to take a fifth academic subject. But the school administration ruled that we'd have to give up gym to do that. Since I was almost a tomboy, I was not happy. Even though there were no team sports for girls, I had enjoyed shooting hoops in gym in the eighth and ninth grades. And I'd worked on my ground strokes in tennis on the asphalt tennis courts a short walk from our house. Who knows? If I'd been allowed to race around a basketball or tennis court, I might have shed a layer of shyness and a pound or two.

As my older siblings peeled away to go to college, our house was no longer a beehive of activity. No more crooning of Ray Charles' smooth voice from the record player in Bud's upstairs bedroom, no more excited chatter while Sue and her friends played Monopoly in the living room. Once the two of them left, Joan got Sue's permission to move into the other spacious bedroom with its pretty prize of a three-quarter wooden-spooled colonial bed. After that, I was wistful. No longer would we whisper confidences between our twin beds. Gone, our nighttime high school gossip about who had a crush on whom, or if Peter might have a glimmer of interest in me.

I was sure that Susan's and Bud's friends had designated me the "little sister," the one whose groaner puns and sharp sarcasm were barely tolerated. It would take years before I honed my sense of humor to overcome shyness and put others at ease. In my teens, I was still testing my skills, aware that sometimes my comments were too sharp-edged.

Like every teenager, I longed to be popular, with girls and boys alike. Now, without Sue, Bud, or Joan's support, I had to get through senior year on my own. One morning before school, staring into the mirror, I ran a finger over a burgeoning blackhead about to spend a week in residence on my chin. Next, my index finger and thumb gravitated to a small wedge around my waist. My smile that I practiced? It looked forced. When I brought up these worries—my few extra pounds, my oily skin, or my fake smile—Mom and Dad brushed them aside.

"That pimple isn't noticeable, Kristin. And it will go away if you leave it alone." Would it? My best friend's older sister had said a month-long Novena, going through the Stations of the Cross, at St. Mary's Star of the Sea Church, asking God for a clear complexion. Her prayers—like my wishes—went unanswered. At least I hadn't wasted hours in that dark and incense-filled church, I consoled myself.

Mom and Dad were like stern gods, never reassuring me that I was pretty. Did they fear it might have gone to my head? Instead, my parents conveyed a philosophy that worrying about popularity and beauty ate up valuable hours. According to them, confident people used talent and intelligence to lead fulfilled lives. At seventeen, I found their outlook hard to live by.

In Beverly, athletics always came before academics. How many towns canvass door-to-door, asking all residents to chip in to send the state Class A football champs with the cheerleaders to Bermuda? When the knock came on our front door, Dad said, "When this town decides to reward the students who excel in their studies, then, and only then, will I consider a donation to the football team." He never wavered. Being characterized in Beverly as "brainy" was the kiss of death, a curse each of us Elliotts dealt with, my siblings more gracefully than me.

It got so bad that Beverly High came close to losing its state accreditation by the time Joan was applying early decision to Mt. Holyoke. At that point, I begged my parents to send me to a boarding school or to a local private day school to prepare for the academic rigor of college ahead. However, paying for four children in six consecutive years to go to college was already a huge investment for Mom and Dad, and even I could do the math. I swallowed hard as they dismissed my pleas. Basically, I had to suck it up, keep my eye on the prize: in one year, I, too, would be a freshman in college.

That was always their mantra: Give it more time. When I had a blackhead, waiting a week for it to clear felt like an eternity. Waiting to graduate, week after week, until fifty-two had ticked by, felt impossible.

During my senior year, there was an event that I wished I could have skipped. Under the hot lights of the center stage of Beverly High School's auditorium, I sat with six other classmates, waiting to accept a woolen blazer for academic excellence. Instead of praising hard work or the virtues of original thinking, our principal gave a ten-minute speech that rambled on about the acceptability of average grades. He assured the assembly, "Getting a C is respectable. After all, I got Cs when I walked these same corridors. Look where I ended up! Top guy! Hey, high grades are overrated."

After the applause, I bolted backstage to my metal locker, yanking off the unflattering black and orange boxy jacket. Its woolen fibers felt prickly under my arms, making me sweat. The bold colors were unflattering against my Celtic skin. I never wore it again.

Looking back, I was a self-critical teenager longing for acceptance and likability. Photographs are not as unkind as my critical eyes that magnified my inferiority. Had I been more forgiving, I'd have realized that even a cheerleader might suffer the indignity of a blemish. I missed Susan, who played games with me. I missed Bud and his friends who teased me out of my self-consciousness. I missed Joan, who had pushed me to ask a crush to dance when it was Ladies' Choice under the twinkling, rotating ball. Without her prodding, I darted into the Ladies' room until the asking was over.

For me, senior year in high school became a waiting game. I was jealous that Joan had escaped. Over weekly phone calls, I heard her enthusiasm: for professors, for classes, for her room-mate Marty, for blind dates at Dartmouth. The Cuban Missile Crisis paralyzed the country over two weeks and hit her campus hard. She asked my parents if she should be home with us, if the Russians were going to blow us all up anyway. Meanwhile, Bud, away at Williams College, told us that his friend Gordie, now in the Coast Guard, was on a warship headed for Cuba. We were all worried for him. Susan, married, lived in western Massachusetts and seemed worlds away. Mostly, we were all afraid during those nerve-racking days in October.

But if we were to die, I would have to do it at home, alone, in my miserable senior year with Joan and Bud and Susan away. Like Susan, our fearless leader, they were in a mysterious collegiate universe, a place that had not opened itself to me. If this was what it was like to be an only child, I was appalled. There was nobody at night to help put the pieces in the puzzle on the card table. There was nobody to watch the *Million Dollar Movie* with or to talk about it afterwards. And no one to help me solve a trigonometry problem. Oddly, I sensed that my parents missed the hubbub as well. My first-grade teacher once had labeled me the "quiet mouse." Certainly, our house was quiet now with only three of us under its roof. Did my parents ever wish that Joan and I had been twins? That way, they'd have had the house to themselves by now.

Unlike my siblings, I did not opt for early decision. A part of me wanted to slip seamlessly into Mt. Holyoke. Another part of me questioned that route. I applied to five prestigious women's colleges because by the spring of 1963, I was tired of educators who denigrated academic achievement and celebrated sports instead. When the admissions director at Mt. Holyoke said, "You know how much we'd love to capture the third Elliott girl.

We'd be excited to have you follow your two sisters." It was my breeziest interview. Family, friends, classmates and teachers assumed my decision would be a slam dunk.

Postponing the decision did not make it any easier. Secretly, I had hoped that the college response envelopes might contain rejections, so that the choice would be narrowed down for me. Instead, all five envelopes were fat, indicating acceptances.

My good fortune was like a curse. Five yeses meant I had simply kicked the can down the road. Maybe I should play Russian Roulette. At night, I'd punch my pillow, considering how Mt. Holyoke would play out. If only Joan were in the opposite twin bed to confide in! Falling asleep, I could hear her voice, reminding me to stand up straighter, to push out my boobs. The next morning, I mailed back my *No, thank you*'s to Skidmore, Smith, and Wheaton. Then came the showdown: Mt. Holyoke versus Wellesley.

On the day of the deadline, I plunked down on the floral print loveseat in the den, Mom's workspace, and sighed. She pushed her ladderback chair from the typewriter to face me. I adjusted my headband before holding up the Holyoke reply card in one hand with its Wellesley counterpart in the opposite. "Eenie, meenie, miney, moe?"

Mom asked, "What's it to be, Kristin? Whichever you pick, it's fine with your father and me. We just want you to be happy." As she rose, I met her halfway.

My voice wobbled. "It's time to strike out on my own, Mom. To make my own way. And not be the last of the Elliotts. Heck, where a teacher doesn't call me by my siblings' name! If I were the third Elliott sister at Mt. Holyoke, I'd have to try to live up to Sue's achievements. And then, I'd have to struggle not to be in Joan's shadow. At Wellesley, I'll be the first and only Elliott. I'll be my own person."

Mom's eyes welled up. She hugged me.

"I understand. You've made your first adult decision. You've had trouble sleeping these past few nights. Now, run down to the mailbox right away before you change your mind. We'll call Joan before supper to tell her your decision."

That evening, hesitatingly, I told Joan my news. "I'm entering the freshman class at Wellesley. They came through with generous scholarship money, too. Please know that this is the hardest decision that I've ever made. Please, please know how it has torn me apart."

I could hear sniffles. Joan, always sensitive, was holding back tears. She said, "I'm disappointed, of course. But glad that you gave it so much thought. You sound pretty sure."

Then, I cried. Was I sure? Of course not.

We knew our relationship was shifting again. I noticed that Mom and Dad were holding hands at the trestle table, listening to Joan's and my conversation. I saw Mom tear up. I had released my Irish twin from her protective charge. I'd be independent, this time by choice. Setting my own course.

I couldn't help but think of the poem we'd read in Mrs. Corbett's junior year English class by the famous New England poet, Robert Frost. The lines from "The Road Not Taken" popped into my mind: "Two roads diverged in a wood, and I— / I took the one less traveled by, and that has made all the difference."

After hanging up the receiver against the kitchen wall, I pushed up the sleeve to my blouse inhaling a whiff from the inside of my elbow. Thanks, Mother Hen, for sharing this comforting secret, along with so many other confidences. I straightened up, thrust out my chest, ready for the less traveled adventure ahead.

ACKNOWLEDGEMENTS

I MULLED THIS BOOK OVER for quite some time before it jelled as a collection of essays about my childhood and adolescence.

While writing snippets under the tentative working title, *Butterscotch or Chocolate*, I met a local writer and poet, Mary Kenny, at the Kemmerer Library in New Vernon, New Jersey. In her early nineties, Mary suggested that we co-lead memoir-writing sessions there. We happily did for a couple of years, and she encouraged me to attend my first writing workshop.

She had attended the year before and raved about it and its locale: Tuscany! It was one of my first trips post-Covid. Sadly, Mary died before I could share my experience with her. In May 2022, under the tutelage of Kathryn Kay and with the feedback from fellow Tuscany workshop attendees, my memoir took shape.

A New Jersey friend that I made at the Italy workshop, Judy Hampson, suggested that we both attend a writing workshop on Hawaii's Big Island in January 2023. There, my writing became more focused. Jill Talbot, my memoir writer/coach, pushed me to expand on what it meant to grow up in a family business named after me. She was enthralled with details that I took for granted. She also suggested that I create a more encompassing book title.

After these two workshops, I realized that I'd better stop packing my bags for exotic locations. It was time to stay home to write! I wanted to treat the upcoming book like a job, setting aside hours every day to write, re-write, and edit. Eventually, by the spring of 2023, this self-discipline got me to a rough manuscript.

Local playwright Joe Vitale, and a dear friend Claire Zweig, made during our serving together on the board of The Shakespeare Theatre of New Jersey, helped me research potential editors. Happily, I zeroed in on René Steinke, a professor of Creative Writing at Fairleigh Dickinson University.

During June and July, René and I worked in sync to reach the final version of *You All Look Alike*. Over that time, I fine-tuned my writing, learning to dig deeper and to express my feelings more clearly. Like Jill, René was fascinated with how much the Kristin Elliott Christmas Card business influenced my siblings and me.

I'd be remiss if I didn't mention that my sister Joan has encouraged me to write creatively ever since my corporate career ended. She was the copy editor for my two earlier books. But this book is too close to the bone to ask that huge favor, despite her generous offer. Additionally, my niece Kristin, my namesake, has been a loyal cheerleader. She possesses a keen interest in our family history. As the oldest of her generation, she had a particularly intimate relationship with my parents, Geem and Geep.

This memoir has been my most challenging book. Why? Because my older siblings will recall the events from their own perspectives. And they'll undoubtedly speak up! Nonetheless, these recollections represent my effort to nail down certain family events for future generations in an engaging manner.

I hope this collection of stories will give our youngest Elliotts insights into their much older family, who lived through two World Wars, the Depression, the Cold War, Vietnam, Watergate, and the Civil Rights movement. My grand-nephew, Marcos, a senior in high school, said before our 2023 summer family reunion, "Aunt Kris, we depend on you because you're the family storyteller."

Thank you, Marcos. You touched my heart. May *You All Look Alike* touch yours.

Made in the USA
Middletown, DE
24 November 2023

43329042R00089